W9-ANB-872

BL
603
.F55

Fingesten, Peter
Eclipse of symbol-
ism

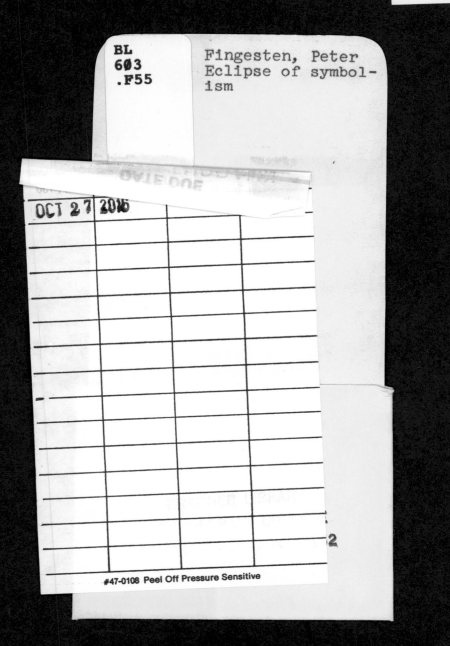

OCT 27 2015

#47-0108 Peel Off Pressure Sensitive

The Eclipse of Symbolism

By the same author / East Is East

Peter Fingesten

THE ECLIPSE OF SYMBOLISM

University of South Carolina Press / *Columbia, S.C.*

BL
603
.F55

704.948
F497e

First Edition
Copyright © 1970 by
The UNIVERSITY OF SOUTH CAROLINA PRESS

Published in Columbia, S.C., by the University of South Carolina Press, 1970

Standard Book Number: 87249–172–2

Library of Congress Catalog Card Number: 77–86194

Manufactured in the United States of America
Composition by Heritage Printers, Inc., Charlotte, North Carolina
Offset lithography by Universal Lithographers, Inc., Lutherville-Timonium, Maryland
Bound by L. H. Jenkins, Inc., Richmond, Virginia

Designed by DAMIENNE GRANT

Contents

Illustrations

ILLUSTRATIONS

Preface

ALTHOUGH PLATO BELIEVED that the planets have souls, and Aristotle that they create the harmony of the spheres, these beliefs have slipped down from accepted truth to symbol, then to metaphor, until, finally, they have lost all meaning in the scientific era. In short, our life is becoming progressively desymbolized since experimental science has detached observed facts from symbolic and mythopoeic interpretations.

The tradition of symbolism connects us to a prehistoric and prescientific mode of thinking. It contributes to a magic world view. Interestingly enough, the belief in symbols began to break down as early as the Neolithic period with the separation of the world into two distinct realms, the Sacred and the Profane. The mystics of all higher religions—like the Hebrew prophets and some Christian mystics and reformers—either cast doubt upon symbols or attacked them outright. During the Italian Renaissance, symbolism became esoteric and fell into the hands of the so-called Illuminati, and later, after the scientific revolution of the seventeenth century, was kept alive by occultists, Romantics, poets, writers, and artists with a special affinity for symbolism.

PREFACE

I have tried to proceed from five case studies of the use of symbolism, which make up the first part of this book, to construct a theory of symbolism which seems to me to manifest the ultimate unsatisfactoriness of symbolism as a verifiable mode of perception. The study of symbols is fascinating. I cannot boast that I am entirely immune to their spell, only that the contemplation of the life of symbols has led, in my case, to the contemplation of their death. I am, no doubt, the child of my time, with its nonobjective art that has broken through traditional art symbols and its experimental science that has rejected all symbolic and allegoric interpretations of phenomena.

But I suspect that I am equally indebted to patristic literature. The *Protrepticus*, *Stromata* and other writings of Clement of Alexandria, in which the Athenian convert found Christian thought superior to the prevalent Greek thought of his day, still suggest a way of criticizing the symbolical view of the world. And St. Augustine continues to lead us beyond symbols to the direct religious experience.

As Alfred North Whitehead wrote in *Symbolism, Its Meaning and Effect*, "The repulsion from symbolism stands out as a well marked element in the cultural history of civilized people. There can be no reasonable doubt but that this continuous criticism has performed a necessary service in the promotion of wholesome civilization, both on the side of the practical efficiency of organized society, and on the side of a robust direction of thought" (quoted in Rollo May, *Symbolism in Religion and Literature* [New York, 1960], p. 233). There is also the danger that the more symbolic the universe one moves in, the further one is removed from reality. The insane live in entirely private symbolic worlds, cut off from reality. Symbols are antiques. Their only reality is as part of the history of religion and art.

Since the Greek Skeptics, anyone who has written about symbolism at all has faced the problem of discussing one symbolic system by means of another system, namely language, that is itself symbolic. Plotinus and St. Augustine, in their different ways, advocated a nonverbal solution to the problem, such as silent aesthetic contemplation or a direct mystical encounter with reality. Experiences which we call "elemental" and which do not involve myths, symbols, or language are available to human beings—experiences such as eating, drinking, and making love. The basis of my criticism of symbols, then, is my conviction that the direct experience of reality is the ideal way of perceiving and comprehending it.

The following essays have been published before but have been edited and regrouped. "Art Motifs as Symbols of Life and Society" and "The Craft of Creation" appeared in *Antaios* (Stuttgart), Fall, 1965, and Fall, 1968, respectively; "The Eye of God" in *Criticism*, Winter, 1959; "The Smile of the Buddha" in *Oriental Art* (London), Autumn, 1968; "Allegories of the Gothic Cathedral" in the *Journal of Aesthetics and Art Criticism*, Fall, 1961; and "The Symbolism of Nonobjective Art" in the *Art Journal*, Fall, 1961. "Symbolism and Allegory" was written for the *Helen Adolf Festschrift* published by Frederick Ungar (New York, 1968). "A Sixfold Schema of Symbolism" was first published in the *Journal of Aesthetics and Art Criticism*, Summer, 1963. "Symbol or Visual Presence?" and "The Eclipse of Symbolism" have not been published before but were written for this book.

Acknowledgments

THE AUTHOR WISHES to express his gratitude to the Committee on Scholarly Research Projects of Pace College, New York, which supported the completion of several chapters of this book.

There are many teachers, colleagues and friends to whom acknowledgment is due, particularly Antoinette K. Gordon, Dr. Helen Adolf, Dr. Marianne Beth, Dr. Edmund E. Tolk, Dr. Sterling A. Callisen, Professor Austin Fowler, Professor Brenda Bettinson, Thomas D. Waller, Patricia Ross Bodine, Dr. Thais Lindstrom, Professor Warren White, and Meryl Stoller.

Special mention is due my wife Faye, without whose critical understanding and assistance in editing and typing no line of mine has ever appeared in print.

1/SYMBOLISM

It is the mark of an educated man to look for precision in
each class of things just so far as the nature of the subject admits
—ARISTOTLE, *Nicomachean Ethics*
1094b, 23–25

Method and theory are not, of course, the same, but it can be said that a
method of analysis is of value only if it produces some advance in
theory, and that an advance in theory is as important as an
exemplification of method as it is in itself—E. E. EVANS-PRITCHARD,
Introduction to Robert Hertz, *Death and the Right Hand*

Art Motifs as Symbols of Life and Society

THE DEGREE OF REALITY a society perceives is expressed and limited by its choice of art motifs. All cultures, from the most primitive to the most evolved, have a fairly rigid preference for specific art motifs which is not due to stylistic reasons alone. Subject matter in all periods seems to be restricted to those motifs needed by society to cope with the surrounding world visually, intellectually, and magically. The history of art demonstrates that art motifs gradually increased in number from the French and Spanish prehistoric caves to the Ancient Near East. An even fuller vocabulary was achieved in Greece and Rome, culminating, at least in quantity and variety, in the Renaissance. After that period, which spans about three centuries, the visual repertory became exhausted during the late nineteenth century, and subject matter was abandoned entirely by the abstract artists of our time.

Primitive societies are the most restricted in their choice of motifs. In discussing the arts of the Australian aborigines, Charles P. Mountford wrote, "All the members of an aboriginal community are artists, the men, the women, and the children. There is no special artist class, although most of the artistic activities belong to the realm of the men. The art motifs are limited and the media few, nevertheless, the aborigines produced simple works of art, some of which have considerable merit. . . . I think the factors limiting the aboriginal artist would be the art motifs of his culture. He would be unlikely to invent an entirely new motif, but would use those with which he was familiar."[1] Plato, contemplating the arts of the Egyptians, noted with approval how they prohibited any innovations in motif or style. "That nation, it would seem, long enough ago recognized the truth we are now affirming, that poses and melodies must be good, if they are to be habitually practised by the youthful generation of citizens. So they drew up the inventory of all the standard types, and consecrated specimens of them in their temples. Painters and practitioners of other arts were forbidden to innovate on these models or entertain any but the traditional standards, and the prohibition still persists, both for these arts and for music in all its branches. If you inspect their painting and reliefs on the spot, you will find that the work of ten thousand years ago—I mean the expression not loosely but in all precision—is neither better nor worse than that of today; both exhibit an identical artistry" (Laws II 656d.).[2]

Plato was so impressed by the continuous tradition of Egyptian art motifs, such as "Pharaoh bringing offering," "Djed ceremony," "Papyrus hunt," and others, that he overlooked their obvious stylistic changes from the Old Kingdom to the New Kingdom and even mistook the archaism of the Late Period for the aesthetic equal of the Old Kingdom. There have been stylistic changes of form in the arts of Egypt and of other cultures, but this is not the subject under consideration here. The specific motifs of a society and the slowly expanding vocabulary of art motifs parallel man's growing awareness of himself and the world.

The variety of art motifs employed throughout art history, however, is so great that this chapter attempts no more than to lay the foundation of an ordering schema of motifs according to their symbolic significance. Since it would be impractical to enumerate and account for every motif that ever made its appearance in the history of art, I propose five major categories of motifs which express the orientation of the society that employed them: (1) Evocative; (2) Invocative; (3) Revealing; (4) Initiating; and (5) Self-initiating.

ART MOTIFS

During the Paleolithic period man lived in caves, which served both as shelters and as places of worship. From his small hollow in a mountain he tried to dominate his whole known cosmos through symbols and images hidden in the dark recesses of his cave. Cro-Magnon man and allied peoples, such as the Grimaldi, lived in an enchanted world without knowledge of cause and effect. They believed that a painting of a pregnant cow or an animal with arrows scratched over its body could effectively influence the course of events. Cro-Magnon man did not simply hope that a small, pregnant Venus statuette would increase his family; he believed that without it the procreation of the tribe was impossible. All he had to do was evoke (call out) the power which resided in the image, or draw the magic sign, and the desired result would occur.

In the evocative arts of the prehistoric caves the mysterious forces of nature were trapped and hostile forces were held at bay. At the Paleolithic level of conceptualization the symbols had as much power as the concepts for which they stood. Indeed, Paleolithic man may not have recognized any difference between symbol and concept. In such images the finite and the infinite overlapped. The image was the only reality perceived, and, in terms of protective magic, that which is visible (and therefore contained) is never as dangerous as that which is invisible.

While murals of animals and hunters or fertility images clearly indicate their purposes, the abstract signs often found in these murals do not. Some scholars have seen them as diagrams of architectural structures, such as tents or corrals, while others have interpreted them as apotropaic devices. Hand prints, prominent in Spanish caves, are also not completely understood. They are often mutilated, indicating that some type of ritual was connected with them. They may also have been symbols of the artist-magicians, like signatures, similar to the thumbprints of illiterates. If found near or superimposed on animal murals, they may have signified domination over the souls of the animals. Among the most intriguing symbols are the dots in the Lascaux caves, which are arranged in groups of two, three, six, or more. Aside from their magical connotation, the fact that they are carefully arranged in groups or series hints at a primitive concept of number. Some geometrical devices, such as the two lozenge patterns with crossbar of the famous Deer and Salmon engraving from the Cave Larthet in France, are so distinct and articulate as to suggest hieroglyphs that have not yet been translated. Evidently the abstract signs and symbols served various purposes; some of them were undoubtedly magical signs, foci of power expected to radiate their magic over the scenes of animals and the hunt near which they were drawn.

To Cro-Magnon man art was a matter of life and death. He was not aware of the aesthetic or formal aspects of his creative efforts, only of attaining the desired effects by the most direct means possible. He identified almost completely with the animals portrayed and could therefore achieve astonishing naturalism. When a hunter was portrayed, however, as in the "Prehistoric Tragedy" of Lascaux, he was represented as an unreal, schematic figure, while the wounded bull attacking him was painted naturalistically, shaded and with his horned head twisted. The portrayal of the individual as an individual does not exist in Paleolithic art. Man was absorbed completely by the cosmic forces he was trying to harness. Even later, in Spanish Paleolithic caves, when hunters achieved more substance, they were usually painted very small in comparison to the overpowering proportions of the animals they are attacking. The Venus statuettes, on the other hand, though highly symbolic in their exaggeration of female characteristics, were based upon close observation of pregnant women. These faceless yet deeply expressive statuettes represented female creativity on a universal level rather than that of any individual human mother.

The incredible power which resides in the arts of prehistoric man can still be felt more than 20,000 years after their creation. Paleolithic man restricted himself to eight types of subject matter: animals, hunters, disguised magicians, Venus statuettes, female figures, decorated weapons, hand symbols, and abstract symbols.[3] They not only corresponded to his level of understanding of the cosmos—they were his cosmos, expressing the all-pervasive magical nature of his life.

The invocative category of art motifs reflects a deeper knowledge of the workings of nature and is vast compared to the limited category of evocative motifs. When man settled down to agricultural pursuits and animal husbandry, he discovered the causal relationship between sowing and harvesting, mating and birth, and he observed the regular occurrence of the seasons and the march

of the stars over the sky. He did not need to place all his faith in the
magical arts as absolutely essential for survival, but he resorted to them for
additional help and assistance in calamities.

The arts of Egypt and Mesopotamia were mainly invocative (call into).
Magic powers did not reside in the images, ipso facto, but had to be invoked
through complicated rituals of consecration, such as the Egyptian "opening of the
mouth" ceremony,[4] and inscriptions of sacred formulae or names. This was the
stage of collaboration between man and the mysterious forces of the cosmos,
whereas during the evocative stage the images had independent power.

The invocative stage marks the discovery of the individual as an individual.
He is portrayed in Mesopotamian and Egyptian reliefs acting and interacting with
other figures, or placed in a natural or architectural setting. Mesopotamian images
of gods, kings, and men are aggressive, projecting their powers outward through
their wide-open, exaggerated eyes, while Egyptian images are calmer and more
idealistic. A carved slave in the grave of an Egyptian aristocrat was just stone, a
painted basket of food was just a painting, until consecration endowed them with
a pseudolife, a ghostly existence between this and the next life. The Egyptian
custom of carving substitute bodies of the deceased in which his shadow
soul, or Ka, could settle was a compromise between magical and aesthetic
values. Art and ritual replaced human sacrifice, at least in the royal graves of
dynastic Egypt, which contain carved and painted slaves who would serve
their masters in the beyond. Had the Egyptians not discovered the symbolic aspects
of art, Egypt could not have achieved the transition from barbarism to
civilization.

Certain consecrated images had the power of conferring immortality upon those
of royal blood. On the underside of the lids of many sarcophagi there was
painted a representation of the sky goddess Nut. When a royal body was
deposited in the sarcophagus and the lid closed, the soul of the deceased was
believed to be received into her celestial realm. As one hymn addressed to Nut
puts it:

> *Great one, who became Heaven,*
> *Thou didst assume power; thou didst stir;*
> *Thou hast filled all places with thy beauty.*

The whole earth lies beneath thee.
Thou hast taken possession of it.
Thou enclosest the earth and all things [on it] in thy arms.
Mayest thou put this Pepi into thyself as an imperishable star.[5]

Another variation reads, "Thy mother Nut spreads herself over thee in her name of Mystery of Heaven, she makes thee to live as a god, and to be without enemies."[6] Invocative art served as mediator between man and the higher powers and between life and death.

Some ornaments and minor arts make their appearance in the Ancient Near East about 3500 B.C. in Egypt and somewhat earlier in Sumeria. These were never intended merely to please the eye. They were made significant, if not symbolic, through the use of decorative elements derived from sacred plants, the sistrum of Isis, the djed column of Osiris, sacred animals, stars, and so forth. Two other important repositories of invocative arts were the grave and the temple. Ancient architecture was entirely sacred, symbolizing rebirth in the case of the grave and proximity to God in the temple. The Pylon temple, a perfect symbol of the Egyptian concept of the cosmos, had a flat ceiling, painted blue with gold stars, floating like the night sky high above the gigantic sacred lotus or papyrus columns which "grew" from the foundation as from the earth. In the twilight of vast temples stood images of the gods or of deified pharaohs ready to assist man in his quest for immortality.

Invocative images are not, however, without aesthetic considerations. Careful execution of grave or temple images preceded consecration rituals. In Egypt many grave sculptures of the deceased were immured, since they were carved not to please the living but to serve as substitute bodies for the Ka, yet their lifelikeness is often remarkable and their execution painstaking. Animals in Egyptian tombs are tenderly and naturalistically represented, indicating an intimacy between man and animals. In the Ancient Near East, architecture, painting, and sculpture emerged as specialized activities and lucrative occupations, and, aside from the ultimate purpose of these arts, pride in workmanship and a striving for personal satisfaction are evident in their technical and aesthetic refinement.

ART MOTIFS

Evocative subject matter has an immediate effect—it is possessed, it *is* the power. Invocative subject matter, on the other hand, while still magical, expresses not immediate but remote effects and is far broader in range and application. Its magical qualities receded in proportion to the increase of aesthetic considerations. The purpose of evocative art motifs was to dominate and influence the course of nature magically; that of invocative motifs was to act as mediator between man and the cosmos, to protect him and to guarantee him immortality.

The revealing category of motifs encompasses all subject matter directed toward presenting a given image of the world. Its main purpose was to teach society the rules of class distinction, the physical appearance of the rulers and gods, certain aspects of ritual, and the appearance of man's surroundings. It is essentially a visual category; great attention was paid to idealization or exaggeration of certain features deemed important to figures of authority. Since the masses of the people never came into the presence of oriental potentates, the temple images or *stelae* taught them how to see and respect their rulers. In many cases, of course, the invocative and revealing aspects coalesced. A temple sculpture of the enthroned Pharaoh Khafre of the Fourth Dynasty served as a substitute body for his Ka, as an idealized representation of himself, and as a symbol of his authority over the people and the land of Egypt.

The well-known Stele of Hammurabi is another example of the revealing aspect of art. It stood in the city of Babylon during his lifetime and clearly had a teaching function. Its upper zone represents the bearded king standing at attention before the seated sun god Shamash, the god of justice. Both are solemn and dressed in the convention of the period. The lower zone displays the famous law code, incised in cuneiform. This stele combines various revealing aspects, such as the physical appearance of the king and god, as well as the code itself for the instruction of the people.

Nature gods of the Egyptian, Mesopotamian, Greek, and Roman pantheons gained in substance through art. The revelation of familiar zoomorphic or anthropomorphic features enabled the people to visualize them better and to focus their petitions and prayers. The Hebrew prohibition against representations of the Divine may be explained, in part, by the tradition that the Supreme God did not reveal himself to Moses on Sinai in a bodily form, and that man would be presumptuous to portray that which no one has ever seen. The multitudes of gods in preclassic and classic art were enlarged projections and idealizations of familiar forms. Greek and Roman citizens did not measure themselves against other men but against their gods, since they represented the highest level of human virtue and perfection. Christian theology hesitated for hundreds of years before it permitted anthropomorphic representations of Christ, the Madonna, and saints; and portrayals of Christ originated relatively late (fourth century A.D.). Christian art learned to straddle the dilemma of representing the invisible Logos by basing itself upon the dogma of the Incarnation. Christian art may be classified as essentially revealing. It becomes invocative only when consecrated and evocative when certain images become imbued with protective, healing, or other virtues.

Another kind of revealing motif is that concerned with royal power. Never has the animal kingdom been portrayed with more attention and brilliance than in Assyrian art. For the first time lions were depicted not as proud symbols of royalty, as in Egypt, but as helpless victims of the dreams of glory of brutal and sadistic kings. Their suffering and strain was portrayed with clinical detachment. It was the sudden discovery of this motif, the revelation of animal psychology, which gave these reliefs their forcefulness. The compassionate revelation of human suffering was a Greek discovery. In the arts of the Ancient Near East men were portrayed stylized and symbolic, while animals, almost without exception, were represented realistically and even with a certain psychological insight, as in the Assyrian palace reliefs. The Greeks extended their powers of observation toward themselves, and thus Greek art discovered the individual, the healthy child of nature reflecting upon his fate. To see man as a unique being was the beginning of the modern view. In late Hellenistic art, portrayals of suicide and of those persecuted by fate appeared; this exaggerated naturalism was probably the direct result of the individual's search for meaning in a cosmos that had become progressively hostile.

The three-dimensional nude and the representation of running or falling soldiers, as well as of athletes moving freely in space, are new additions by Greek sculptors to the revealing category of motifs. This category also includes illusionistic still lifes, genre, and the study of the landscape for its own sake. Pompeian mosaics and frescoes presented nature in depth, with linear perspective and shadows. After the hiatus of over 1,000 years of Christian art which was more interested in the revelation of the ideal features of the sacred figures, the Italian Renaissance rediscovered nature once more. In Venetian painting the landscape competes with man and often overpowers him. On the one hand, the Italian Renaissance raised man to the level of a hero, and the "individual as a work of art" dominated his background aggressively, as in the portraits by Antonello da Messina, Botticelli, or Piero della Francesca. On the other hand, he recedes like an object among objects or shrinks to insignificance in the landscapes of Giorgione, El Greco, and the Dutch landscapists of the seventeenth century. Nature became as much a revelation of character and inner meaning as were portraits of saints, heroes, and women. The revealing category of motifs was the first category without magic; every new visual dimension is a further discovery of reality.

To Renaissance artists, and to artists ever since, the choice of subject matter has been an expression of freedom. No subject was to be treated with reservation—on the contrary, the scientific study of man and nature became desirable. The countless new motifs which emerged enabled man to stand back, to contemplate, and to measure himself against them. We must not forget that certain scientific theories could be understood only by the most learned men. The theory that the world is round, for instance, could not be visualized except by a few highly trained cartographers and mathematicians. But when art employed chiaroscuro and linear perspective, depth could be experienced visually, and in this way the acceptance of a new scientific idea by the masses was facilitated. The great Renaissance theoretician Leon Battista Alberti implied this in his book *On Painting*. "As for me, I certainly consider a great appreciation of painting to be the best indication of a most perfect mind, even though it happens that this art is pleasing to the uneducated as well as to the educated. It occurs rarely in any other art that what delights the experienced also moves the inexperienced."[7]

The fourth category of art motifs deals with death—initiation into the mysteries of death. Art and death may seem antagonistic to each other, for one stands for life and creativity and the other for the termination of creativity. Yet the two have an alliance that goes back to the beginning of art. The earliest known appearance of this connection is in the so-called "Prehistoric Tragedy" of the Lascaux caves, the largest and most ambitious mural of which is that of a wounded bull attacking a disguised priest who falls over backwards, paralyzed by the powerful blow. The mural was, no doubt, based upon a real event which impressed itself traumatically upon the artists and members of the Cro-Magnon hunting band which created this scene. From stiff portraits of Old Kingdom nobles waiting in rapt attention upon their fate, relaxed nude youths of classic Greek grave stelae, nervous and fearful Hellenistic representations of the deceased, to Roman grave portraits with drilled pupils which stare into the distance trying to guess their fate, all the arts associated with the grave reflect society's attitude toward death.

The two motifs that have moved mankind more than any others during the last two thousand years are the Crucifixion and the Buddha. The realization that even God had to die makes our fate much easier to bear. These images are not only reminders of death but are also educational. The two largest religions of mankind teach that death is not total extinction, that it leads to either the Resurrection or Nirvana. The West accepts suffering as a path to grace and confronts us with images of the body on the cross. The East prefers to see Buddha smiling, contemplating Nirvana and understanding that life and death have neither meaning nor fear. Even the concept of eliminating death by overcoming it keeps it constantly before the eyes of Buddhists through the images of Buddha. The Crucifixion and the Buddha reconcile death with life. To Christians, the event on the cross is the great death which absorbs and neutralizes individual death. This applies to Buddhism as well, for if Buddha's message is understood from the images, fear and anxiety will vanish. These motifs thus make the unbearable bearable.

Art, in depicting death, also celebrates life. Creativity itself forestalls death, and every work of art, at least in the more individualistic West, is a monument to its creator. This applies particularly to the pyramids and to Greek and Roman mausolea which, besides being graves, celebrate the power of their creators, and their will to be remembered. Every creative act is a death-negating act.

ART MOTIFS

Biological life cannot be prolonged through art, but its limitations can be overcome, to a certain extent, by the stamp of eternity that artists hope to place upon their works. As Berdyaev, the great Russian philosopher, wrote, "It is the tragedy of creativeness that it wants eternity and the eternal, but produces the temporal and builds up culture which is in time and part of history. The creative act is an escape from the power of time and ascent to the divine."[8]

As we have seen, the ever-expanding vocabulary of art motifs has aided man's expanding consciousness of himself, of nature, and of the cosmos. But in the last few hundred years science has made such enormous advances that it has preempted the arts in the role of assisting, teaching, and initiating man. Traditional art motifs have steadily crumbled away. The last significant religious paintings were produced in the seventeenth century. During the eighteenth century the last portrayals of man as the proud center of the cosmos were painted, and in the nineteenth century, after its short-lived Classic and Romantic periods, art finally turned to nature divested of God and man with the work of the Realists and the Impressionists. When figures or nudes appear in the art of the second half of the nineteenth century, they are treated as painterly subjects rather than as revelations of deeper humanistic or spiritual significance.

The new dimensions which have caught the imagination of twentieth-century man are scientific. Into what insights of a chemical, biological, or atomic nature can art initiate us? The experiments of certain artists with new media and new techniques are attempts to forestall being left behind by scientific advances. But still, art cannot and should not compete with atom smashers, astronauts, or radio astronomy. As a reaction, art retreated into itself to discover frontiers not crossed by science. It has attained the stage of self-initiation into the unexplored inner cosmos. Interestingly enough, the further scientists look into stellar and interstellar spaces, the further artists look within themselves.

Nineteenth-century Symbolists and early twentieth-century Surrealists only touched the surface of the subconscious with their transfiguration of known visual data. They surrounded the world with the chiaroscuro of their dreams, yet they did not accomplish a deep penetration into further dimensions of the psyche. That was left to nonobjective art, with its entirely new and mysterious world of formal and spiritual symbolism dealing with inner spiritual tensions rather than a rearrangement of dream fragments. Nonobjective art is visual prophecy; it delineates worlds as yet undiscovered and dimensions as yet unseen.

Nonobjective art is a style, in spite of the formal extremes represented by Mondrian and Kandinsky, stripped of all associative elements, until all that is left upon the canvas is the raw creative process. This creative process is different from that of the past. The painter does not create with preconceived symbols, objects, or sketches but allows his creativity to guide him. As the Abstract Expressionist painter Hans Hofmann expressed it: "I am often asked how I approach my work. Let me confess: I hold my mind and my work free from any association foreign to the act of painting."[9] In this approach there is the possibility of a more direct revelation of psychic processes than past approaches afforded. An abstract artist contemplates his work with as much wonder as any onlooker and searches his own work for clues. Nonobjective art has had to reject not only all appearances of the outer world but also all traditional symbolism as inadequate for the new dimensions toward which it is groping. What traditional motifs and symbols are adequate to convey the mysterious unnamed regions of the psyche? It is the mysticism of nonobjective art rather than its forms that shocks.

In nonobjective art, at least in its best examples, the artist communes with that aspect of himself which is nearest to eternity. Mondrian sacrificed the human dimension only to participate in a superhuman one. In rejecting the traditional art motifs and symbols we have discovered the importance of the creative act in our time. We are surrounded by works of art that convey no known symbols, have no purpose other than their own existence, and are, in the main, explorations into the creative process and into the inner self—in other words, self-initiations. The art motifs chosen by a society are the symbols of that society's concept of reality, and every culture and time has its own grammar of motifs. Artistic creation can be compared to war with the unknown, with nature, with death and extinction, in which the sum of all the art motifs of every society is a victorious campaign in the unending struggle.

The Craft of Creation

THE MOST ANCIENT METAPHOR which made comprehensible the miracle of the creation of life was that of a god creating man from clay or stone. In creation myths from Greece to India there are stories of a god who created animals or men in the same manner as a sculptor would create a figure. Long before philosophy and writing existed, artists had firmly impressed society with their powers of creating lifelike images. They were believed to have magical powers and were probably feared. As Plato expressed it in the Timaeus, in ancient predeluvian Athens the caste of artificers did not intermix and lived apart from the other castes of priests and shepherds and hunters.[1] This idea is based, no doubt, upon the tradition of guild secrets and organization which go back to prehistoric times.

Artists (potters, painters, sculptors, and architects) were specialists in all known cultural periods. This can be traced from the Paleolithic period,[2] the Ancient Near East until today. As early as the fifth millennium B.C., the potter-specialist of Arpachiah occupied a dominant position in his village. "The most important building was a spacious house, standing in the center of the Tepe. . . . This was the largest house discovered on the site [T.T.6, Tell-Halaf period]. This house, which alike by its situation and size was clearly the property of one of the headmen in the village, proved to have been the workshop of a potter and the maker of stone vases and of flint and obsidian tools. . . . All the objects found in this house displayed the elegance of finish which is the hall-mark of the master craftsman. It is significant, therefore, that this place of manufacture lay in the very center of Arpachiah. . . . We might, in fact, guess that the stone carver and painter at Arpachiah had as a class singled themselves out."[3]

To at least one historical artist fell the honor of deification. Imhotep, the architect of the Third Dynasty who built the step pyramid for Pharaoh Dzozer, was elevated to the position of protecting deity of scribes, artisans, and artists. Daedalus, the great Greek sculptor and architect, mythological builder of the labyrinth at Knossos, is based, no doubt, like other artists thus singled out in ancient mythologies, upon the memories of historical figures who have the quality of culture-heroes. In this sense the Hindu god Vishmakarman, the Vedic "architect of the universe," revealed the science of architecture and mechanics. In the Mahabharata he is described as "the lord of the arts, executor of a thousand handicrafts, the carpenter of the gods, the most eminent of artisans," and "in the late Puranas he is also represented as having made the great wooden image of Jaganatha (a form of Krishna) at Puri."[4]

The analogy between the craftsmen who create images from clay or stone and a god who creates men from the same material was compelling. It occurs in several creation myths. In the Old Testament, for instance, we read: "And the LORD God formed man of the dust of the ground, and breathed into his nostrils the breath of life; and man became a living soul" (Gen. 2:7). According to this version man was first modeled out of clay which was previously moistened by mist (Gen. 2:6). The first man was as yet only a sculpture of clay in the image of God. Only after he was modeled did he receive the spirit of God and become a living soul. This theory of creation derives from a craft tradition; according to Theodore Gaster, "the Hebrew word [create] appears to denote properly 'to cut' and thence possibly 'to chisel, shape.' "[5] Even the name "Adam" is derived from "ground," probably red ground or ceramic clay.[6] And the "breathing in of the spirit" suggests pottery making. Baked pottery has to be hollowed out to prevent it from exploding in the firing process, and the act of "breathing in" is logically conceivable only with hollow clay images or vessels. Both "clay" and "vessel" were biblical metaphors for man. "But now, O LORD thou art our father; we are the clay, and thou our potter . . ." (Isa. 64:8); "I am forgotten as a dead man out of mind; I am like a broken vessel" (Psalm 31:12).

In the ancient home of the Hebrews, Mesopotamia, earth and clay were thought of not as dead matter but as animated. Ninhursaga, the personification of the earth, was therefore addressed as "Mother Earth," queen of the gods, and lady of the mountains. In another aspect the earth was Nintu, "the lady who gives birth"; she was also Níg-zi-gál-dím-me, "the fashioner of everything wherein is the breath of life."[7]

Pottery has rightly been declared a criterion for civilization, and the potter's wheel the implement that led to specialization and mass production. In the Uruk period the wheel, operated by professional potters, came into use throughout Mesopotamia.[8] In this connection it is important to note that these were usually male specialists, no longer women for whom potting, as V. Gordon Childe puts it, "is just a household task like cooking and spinning."[9] The specialized male potter undoubtedly contributed to the conception of a male god who "created" man either by hand (Yahweh) or on the pottery wheel (Khnemu) from a material considered the source of life. (Fig. 1)

In Mesopotamia the religion of the Hebrews was as yet not distinguished by the ethical monotheism it was to achieve after the Exodus (Josh. 24:2). Every home had one or several statues representing ancestors, the so-called teraphim. These images were made of a variety of materials, such as silver and wood, but the majority were of clay. Teraphim were considered gods and were worshiped. Besides oracular consultation, the form of worship seems to have consisted of kissing, stroking, and prostration.[10] That teraphim were thought of as gods is confirmed by the story of Jacob's flight from Laban, when Rachel stole her father's teraphim (Gen. 31:19, 30). "And Laban went to shear his sheep; and Rachel had stolen the images that were her father's." "And now, though thou wouldest needs be gone, because thou sore longedst after thy father's house, yet wherefore hast thou stolen my gods?"

Even in the period after the exile teraphim were popular. We read that, when

1 Khnemu Shaping Man on the
Pottery Wheel. After E. A. Wallis
Budge, *The Gods of the Egyptians*
(London, 1904)

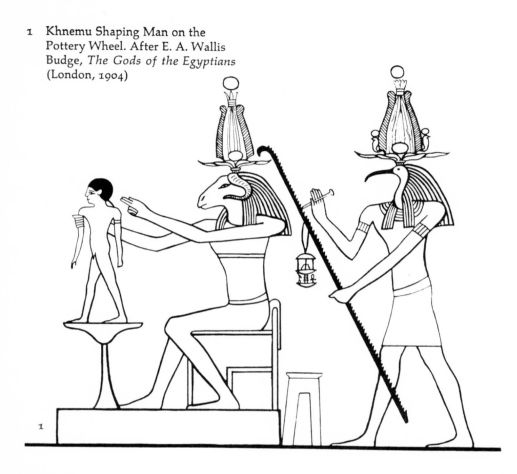

1

David escaped from Saul, Michael placed a life-size (!) teraphim in his bed
which passed for his body (I Sam. 19:13). Some teraphim were installed in
temples, and a priest was appointed to conduct the ritual (Judg. 17:3–5).
On two occasions the dead are termed "Elohim," or gods (I Sam. 28:13; Isa.
8:19), and the difference between the departed spirits and gods, and ancestors
and teraphim, was not yet recognized. "Evidently the teraphim cult was
practically on a plane with YHWH (Yahweh) worship."[11] Clay figures of ancestors

became equated with gods among the Hebrews. The story of the creation of man in Genesis 2:7 represents the anthropomorphic God as creating the ancestor of all ancestors, Adam, out of clay. Does this mean that Adam was the first teraphim, and that the first potter or sculptor was raised to the level of a creating divinity, a type of demi-urge?

The Gilgamesh epic is the earliest literary account of the creation of a living being from clay. It dates from about 2000 B.C. but probably goes even farther back to various Sumerian sources. Gilgamesh was originally a historical personage whom the Sumerian king list assigns to the First Dynasty of Ur.[12] The crucial lines in the Gilgamesh epic relate that the valiant Enkidu, friend of the hero, was created by Aruru from "pinched-off clay."[13] This was the forerunner of the Genesis account of the creation of man, as Enkidu was created in the image of the highest god. There is a remarkable coincidence in the fact that Gilgamesh was king of Uruk when the pottery wheel, operated by professional potters, had spread throughout Mesopotamia and sculptors had emerged as specialized craftsmen.

Another creation myth of the first Babylonian dynasty, unfortunately recovered only in fragments, relates that the goddess Mami (Ninhursag), at the behest of Enki (Ea), created man from clay mixed with the blood of a slain god.

> *Enki opened his mouth*
> *And said to the great gods:*
> *"In the month of substitution (?) and help,*
> *Of the purification of the land (and) the judgment of its shepherd,*
>
> *Let them slay a god,*
> *And let the gods . . .*
> *With his flesh and his blood*
> Let Ninhursage mix clay,
> God and Man
> *. . . united (?) in the clay."*[14]

Sumerian pottery and clay images antedate the written Hebrew and Babylonian creation epics by about 2,000 and 1,000 years respectively. The Hebrews received the teraphim cult from "neighbors." In Genesis 35:2–4

teraphim are called "strange gods," and Ezekiel 21:21 describes the king of
Babylon standing at the crossroads using teraphim for divination. This comes
very close to the use of teraphim among the Hebrews, who, during their
repeated contacts with the superstitious people of Mesopotamia, adopted from
them the belief in clay images and divination. (Fig. 2)

In Greek mythology we find additional evidence that a preliterate artistic
tradition could very probably have influenced myths of the origin of mankind.
There are several examples of the creation of man through the plastic arts.
Prometheus created the race of men in the image of the gods from clay moistened
with river water, while Athene, the goddess of wisdom, breathed in the divine
spirit. At the bidding of Zeus, Haephestus shaped Pandora, the first woman,
from clay. These Greek myths recall both the Gilgamesh epic and the Genesis
account and suggest a Mesopotamian diffusion. But there is another myth,
entirely original, which proves that the presence of earlier unexplained stone
sculptures can give rise to an etiological creation myth.

The Deucalion myth tells that, after the flood with which Zeus sought to
exterminate the race of man during the age of Men of Bronze, only two pious
people survived, Deucalion and his wife Pyrrha. They were saved in a boat
that landed on the highest mountain, Parnassus. Lonely upon the barren earth,
Deucalion exclaimed to his wife, "Oh, how I wish my father Prometheus
had taught me the art of creating man and breathing spirit into shapes of clay."
They pleaded before the altar of Themis for help in re-creating the vanished
race of men. A voice replied, "Veil your heads, loosen your garments, and cast
the bones of your mother behind you." At first Deucalion did not understand
these mysterious words, but faith in the divine command illuminated his mind:
the mother meant the earth, and her bones meant the stones. "And the stones—
who would believe it?—began at once to lose their hardness and stiffness,
to grow slowly, and softened to take on form. Then, when they had grown
in size and become milder in their nature, a certain likeness to the human form,
indeed, could be seen, still not very clearly, but such as statues just begun
out of marble have, not sharply defined, and very like roughly blocked-out
images."[15]

The Deucalion myth of the creation of mankind from stones reminds one

2 Assyrian Ancestor Idol. Khorsarabad,
Paris, Louvre

3 Cycladic Idol. Private Collection,
New York

2   3

of the ancient stone images of Greece with which the invading Northern tribes
became familiar between c. 1500 and 1000 B.C. The Cycladic Islanders were
stone carvers and stone worshipers. Wherever they traded, and they traded
vigorously after 3000 B.C., they left their little stone images behind.[16] Ovid's
words, "statues just begun out of marble . . . , not sharply defined, and very like
roughly blocked-out images," are a fair description of the featureless,
abstract stone images of the prehistoric population of Greece. (Fig 3) The
stone-throwing episode of Deucalion and his wife seems to be based upon the
observation of surviving stone idols rather than upon the diffusion of a clay
tradition from Mesopotamia or the sophisticated artifacts of Crete.

The Egyptians visualized the god Khnemu (Khnum), "the builder of gods and
men," as shaping man on a pottery wheel. Khnemu, the first member of the
Elephantine triad, recalls the predynastic period, according to Sir E. A. Wallis
Budge. "It is probable that Khnemu was one of the gods of the pre-dynastic
Egyptians who lived immediately before the dynastic period. . . ."[17] This period,
with its powerful sculptures, never ceased to excite the imagination of the
Egyptians and inspired a creation theory similar to that in Mesopotamia and

THE CRAFT OF CREATION

Greece, except that the potter's wheel was the mechanical aid in the creation of man. As a matter of fact, in one hymn Khnemu is addressed as "patient artist."[18] Henry Frankfort, commenting on this god in another context, writes, "at Elephantine it was said that Khnum, who appeared as a ram, had made all living beings on a potter's wheel, a detail which remains an enigma."[19]

The potter's wheel as an aid in the creation of man remains an enigma only so long as one disregards the antecedence of art to literature and the influence of ancient craft traditions on the conceptualization of the creation of man. There is considerable literary and archaeological evidence that in the Ancient Near East, as well as in Greece, potters and sculptors became the models for a creating god. The creative act either proceeds by hand, with the aid of a potter's wheel, or seems influenced by the presence of unexplained stone sculptures, as in the Deucalion myth. In other words, the ancients considered divine creation a craft.

The concept of the divine artist permeates our culture through the Judeo-Christian tradition, which absorbed the concept from the Mesopotamians and from Greek philosophy since Plato. The wonder of artistic creation became the prototype of divine creation. Artists in turn, then, could identify with God. The prerogative of creation does not belong to God alone; it belongs to all artists. But artists could not have thought of themselves as godlike if God had not been thought of before as a potter or sculptor. Or, as Sir Herbert Read expressed it: "We might say, how could man ever have conceived of a god if he had not first discovered a godlike creativity in himself?"[20]

The Eye of God

THE EYE IS THE BRIDGE between outer and inner reality. To the artist it is the mirror of external reality, and to the poet it is the mirror of the soul. The open eye is symbolic of life and intelligence; closed, it symbolizes sleep and death. It is a symbol of the sun and in some religions of God. The first act after death is to close the eyes of the deceased. Though it is rooted in ancient fears of the evil eye, this gesture symbolically shuts the windows of the soul.

In the process of individuation, primitive man gradually impressed his own image upon nature. Self-discovery, which came before the discovery of nature, led him to identify her mysterious forces with human characteristics. In this process the seeing eye of man was projected into the sky to become the all-seeing eye of God. By a leap of symbolic thinking, the sun, the preeminent "eye of the sky," was assigned human properties and thus became one of the visual symbols of the power of God.

As early as the Pyramid texts, the eyes of Horus represented the sun and the moon, his white right eye the sun, and his black left eye the moon.[1] In Iranian mythology, Mithra is the "ruler of the day sky" and the "watcher of everything upon the world." He is the "Heavenly Light" and represents heat and life. This Persian Lord of Light was worshiped by Roman soldiers as the Invincible Sun.[2] Hindu philosophy also demonstrates clearly the process of identification of the human eye with the sun, the celestial eye. In a discussion of the creation of the four worlds by the cosmic person (Brahma), the Aitareya Upanishad states: "Eyes were separated out; from the eyes, sight [*caksus*]; from sight, Aditya [the Sun]."[3] The sun is believed to be Brahma,[4] and the sun resides in the human eye. "That Person who is seen in the eye—He is the Self [Atman]. . . . That is Brahma."[5]

Greek mythology characterized Zeus as the "all-seeing eye" which ranged to "infinity, all-round about, surveying all the universe."[6] According to Ovid, the sun is equated with "eyes which behold all things."[7] There, too, we find the identification of the eye, the sun, and God. Argus was conceived by the Greeks as possessing one hundred eyes all over his body.[8] He was the watcher who only closed two eyes at a time, possibly a mythological representation of the night sky with its appearing and disappearing stars. Argus suggests the Tibetan god Avalokiteshvara, the god of mercy. This all-seeing god is represented with multiple heads whose "thousand pairs of eyes" look in every direction.[9]

There is a distinct analogy between the sun, the celestial eye which can either create life or destroy it, and the human eye, which is able not only to behold but also to curse. The ancient belief that some people are endowed with the evil eye is echoed in mythology and art. Balor, an ancient Irish mythological figure, king of the giants, had only one eye, which killed whatever it looked upon. And Medusa, queen of the Gorgons, had the power to kill those who beheld her grotesque face. The mask of Medusa, in its awesome or idealized form, was used in Greece to avert the evil eye.[10] The eye is a symbol to express the hidden powers of the individual and the supernatural vision of God. (Fig. 4)

In art, eyes are an integral part of the expressive possibilities of the human face, but before the various types of eyes and their symbolism are dealt with in more detail, those styles which have omitted them altogether should be mentioned. In some Paleolithic carvings of mother goddesses (Venuses of Lespugue and Willendorf) eyes are conspicuous by their absence. Their oval

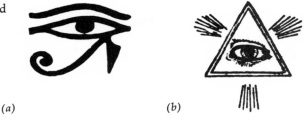

(a)   (b)

heads are bent forward, and, but for a slight indication of hair, they lack any
suggestion of a face. They are blind. What the prehistoric artists wanted to
express is centered not in the face or eyes which are absent, but in the exaggerated
female characteristics of their pregnant bodies. These blind statuettes seem
to reveal a different concept of life and creativity than that developed by later
sedentary cultures. We believe that these blind Venuses represent the anonymous
forces of procreation. At that remote time the individual merged completely
into the life of the tribe, and the contribution of the male toward the creation
of new life may not have been recognized. Paleolithic mother goddesses stand
blind and mute while the creative forces of nature act through them without
regard for individual will. Cycladic idols, though they have long stylized noses,
are also eyeless, and therefore blind. Their exact significance in religious
worship has not yet been established, but there seems to be a connection with
the blind fertility goddesses of an earlier epoch.

The appearance of eyes in art indicates a long process of individuation and
a belief in the inner powers of the personality. In Egyptian art, eyes were
exaggerated to such a degree that without them most sculptures would lose
their majestic appearance. The Egyptian eye is conventional. The heavy upper
lids carefully overlap the lower lids. The eyes are drawn out to the temples,
which gives them their typical almond shape. (Almonds are worn traditionally
as amulets against the evil eye in Italy. In view of the fact that eyes are almond
shaped, this may be a corroboration of the ancient belief that "like influences
like." In Sir James Frazer's terminology this is called the "Law of Similarity"
or "Imitative Magic."[11]) The eyelids of Old Kingdom sculpture have sharp edges
to catch highlights, and they distinctly frame the oval eyeball. In many cases
the head and eyes are slightly tilted up to convey the fixed stare into eternity.

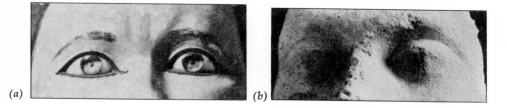

(a)   (b)

To an Egyptian the image of his king was not dead stone but "alive." In fact, every piece of sacred sculpture was believed to contain a spark of the divine, that is, a spark of the god Ptah. The dedication ceremony of a finished temple or tomb sculpture involved the "opening of the mouth" ceremony in the name of Ptah, who was immanent in every creation. "He made their [the gods'] bodies [statues] resemble that which pleased their hearts (that is, the forms in which they desired to be manifest). And so the gods entered into their bodies of every kind of wood, of every kind of stone, of every kind of clay, of every kind of thing which grows upon him, in which they have taken form."[12] The great emphasis upon portraiture with its exaggerated open eyes was expressive of the divine life that imbued every consecrated image. After consecration it could partake of food offered to the Ka and stared into eternity as if the open eye could actually see Duat, the mythical dwelling of the dead.

By way of contrast, New Kingdom sculpture shows an entirely different treatment of eyes. Ikhnaton and Nefertete, enemies of magic and polytheism, who elevated God above themselves to universal grandeur, were represented more naturalistically, with milder expressions. Certain heads of Ikhnaton in particular show the eye only as an oval swelling. The heavy upper lid is articulated, while the lower lid disappears into the softness of his cheek. The eyelids were painted, but the absence of sharp edges gave the eyes an extreme mildness—one might say kindness. (Fig. 5)

It can be stated almost axiomatically that when a magic world view prevailed at a given period, eyes were highly exaggerated, and when magic gave way to science, humanism, or monotheism, as during the Eighteenth Dynasty, eyes were treated with less exaggeration.

Two different treatments of eyes in Egypt have been discussed, in terms of the contrast between Old Kingdom exaggeration and New Kingdom understatement. Greek art offers ample opportunity to compare the treatment of eyes. Taking three random examples from three different stylistic phases—an archaic Apollo, a fifth-century head, and a Hellenistic head—we find that the archaic Apollo has bulging, extremely sharply outlined eyes; the fifth-century head has almost expressionless, mild eyes; and the Hellenistic portrait has focused eyes with penetrating, indented irises. Before Greek philosophy settled down to a rational world view, as represented by the fifth-century Stoa, a magic world view prevailed. The reality of the polytheistic pantheon was taken seriously, and burial and after-death beliefs had a strong influence on the thinking of the people. Superstitions were widely held, and the orgiastic aspects of Dionysian rituals were universally practiced. With the dawn of the fifth century, philosophical criticism made tremendous inroads into popular beliefs, and, instead of magic, humanism and science, as well as a bemused tolerance of the ancient gods, prevailed. At that time Greek art achieved a detached serenity which it possessed neither before nor after. The treatment of eyes was such that our attention is not drawn to them. They are there, but they form an unobtrusive part of the face. The disinterest in the problems of the soul made itself felt by this almost casual treatment of eyes.

After Skopas, eyes became an increasingly prominent feature of the face, until the outlined irises and drilled pupils draw our attention irresistibly to them. When Greece returned to magic and Eastern mystery cults, after Alexander the Great, it lost its serenity not only in life but also in art. Therefore, the Hellenistic eye is exaggerated and penetrating, trying to overwhelm the beholder with its power. In contrast to fifth-century idealized heads, Hellenistic

(a)   (b)

"artists developed portraiture to a point where not only the outer appearance of individuals, but also their spiritual and psychological inner life was reflected."[13] (Fig. 6)

In the archaic Apollos, the eyes are exaggerated and "moving" in their intensity, while the body positions are stiff. During the fifth century the bodies became the carriers of expression through their supple poses and freedom of movement, while the eyes retreated to a relatively unimportant place within the total expression of the figure. Hellenistic art carried to the extreme both the positions of the body and the exaggeration of the eyes, for the tragic mood and magic world view had overtaken Greek thinking.

The most interesting, and perhaps the earliest, representations of detached eye idols are amulets discovered by Max E. L. Mallowan at Brak (1937–1938), the capital of the ancient Habur Valley in northeastern Syria. They were found under the palace in the Jamdat Nasr level and can thus be dated 3100–3000 B.C. Among these strange little amulets (1½ x 2½″), carved in stone, alabaster, and steatite, were some with inlaid and painted eyes, some with double pairs of eyes, and some with elaborate hairdos. In view of their small size and of the fact that several of them are pierced to accommodate a string or leather thong to be tied around the neck, they were probably counter-charms against the evil eye, an interpretation by no means unanimously endorsed among archaeologists but supported by Mallowan himself. "A possible interpretation is that these idols represented an evil eye and were intended to avert other evil eyes from harming the precincts of the building [in which they were found]. But behind all this lies a deep and hidden magic, the purpose of which we can only faintly apprehend. . . ."[14] (Fig. 7)

6 Greek Eyes. (a) Archaic Apollo, VII Century B.C. (b) Male Deity (Zeus?), V Century B.C. (c) Head of Barbarian, Late Hellenistic. Courtesy The Metropolitan Museum of Art, New York

(c)

The eye idols from Brak are tremendously exaggerated; the eyebrows are negatively carved, the eyelids heavy, the eyeballs bulging, and the pupils gouged out. The expression conveyed by these small charms is one of concentrated power, and they have an almost hypnotic stare. Perhaps the exaggeration of the eyes is an effort to convey to the "thrower of the evil eye" (cf. Italian: *jettatore*) that another, equally potent eye, though it is made of stone or clay, protects the wearer. This seems to confirm the ancient belief that magic can be overcome only by stronger magic. A widespread Babylonian magical practice was to tie large clay images of disease-producing demons upon the bodies of the sick in the hope that the demons would be put to flight by the sight of their bound images.[15] And this practice was not confined to the Ancient Near East; in Rome a similar belief gave rise to a similar custom. The golden bulla, a small round or heart-shaped box containing a charm against the evil eye (*fascinum*, or phallus), was worn around the neck by free-born Roman children. This amulet, called by Juvenal "the Etruscan bulla," was removed when boys assumed the *toga virilis*, but it was then dedicated to the *Lares* and hung up over the hearth.[16]

These, of course, are not the only instances in which art has been employed to ward off evil. It is sufficient to recall the guardian animals in front of Egyptian temples, the gargoyles on Gothic churches, and some religious medals which are of an unmistakably apotropaic nature. It is possible that all dot and ring patterns are derived from the eye and thus serve as amulets against the evil eye or, synonymously, envy (*invidia*).

Fear of the evil eye was one of the most universal superstitions of the Mesopotamian people. One exorcism against the evil eye reads as follows:

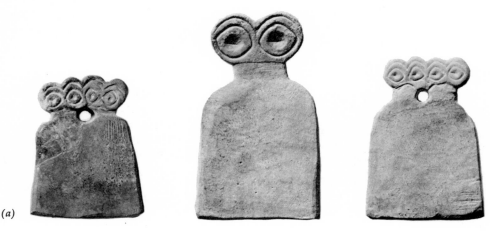

(a)

Thou man, son of his god,
The Eye which hath looked upon thee for harm,
The Eye which hath looked upon thee for evil . . .
May Ba'u smite it with flax (?),
May Gunura [smite it] with a great oar (?)
Like rain which is let fall from heaven,
Directed unto earth,
So may Ea, king of the Deep, remove it from thy body."[17]

The Mesopotamian people were guided in their daily affairs by the earliest and most explicit of law codes. Materialistically inclined, and yet superstitious, they were surrounded by the most extensive demonology known to mankind. They were victims of magicians who exploited their fears of the evil eye and other imaginary dangers with countless amulets, incantations, and exorcisms. In this connection it is interesting that most Mesopotamian representations of men, kings, and gods are distinguished by two characteristics that bear close resemblance to the eye idols at Brak—the exaggerated, bulging eye with sharp eyelids and hollowed or inlaid pupils, and negatively carved eyebrows, joined together. Remarkably enough, these two details cut across all the successive Mesopotamian styles, from the Predynastic to the Sassanian period. The "magic eyes" of Brak seem to be the origin of the typical stylistic formula for eyes in Mesopotamian art, thus linking over 3000 years of artistic production in the Euphrates-Tigris region.

(b)

7 Sumerian Eyes. (a) From Brak, 3100–3000 B.C. (b) Gypsum Figure from Tell Asmar, Late XXVII Century B.C. Courtesy The Metropolitan Museum of Art, New York

We have seen that the open eye, whether exaggerated or not, indicates power. The eye of Medusa kills; that of the Etruscan war god Mars scares; the eye idols from Brak protect against the evil eye; and the mild eyes of Gothic madonnas convey the power of love. Open eyes symbolize the projection of the powers of the soul outward. Half-closed or closed eyes, on the other hand, symbolize the retraction of the soul inwards.

Typical examples of closed eyes are found in the sacred arts of the East. Most of the icons of Hinduism and Buddhism have half-closed or closed eyes. One may state generally that the East, until recent times, was interested not in sight to master nature, but in insight to master the self. The techniques of meditation which are practised in one form or another by most Hindu and Buddhist sects do not permit involvement in the world without. That is the reason most Hindu and Buddhist divinities are shown with closed eyes, lost in rapt meditation. When eyes are shown closed in Western art, they symbolize sleep, suffering, or death. Crucifixions with closed eyes symbolize the death of the flesh. In the East, closed eyes also symbolize death, but only externally—that is, death to life in society. The Buddhist ideal is to overcome the temptations of life, preferably in a monastery, removed from the demands of active participation. The rejection of the world, so typical of the religions of the East, demanded an iconographic formula which, with its closed eyes, expressed it perfectly.

Hindu or Buddhist divinities are not blind. Their eyes are closed to indicate inwardness and isolation, but the icons have a substitute eye on the forehead

45

between the eyebrows. This may be an indentation, a circle, a dot, an inset
stone, or a protuberance. This "third eye," called *ūrnā* or "divine eye," is a
sign of "spiritual insight."[18] (Fig. 8) Though the eyes are closed, the Buddha is
able, through his spiritual powers, to penetrate into the essence of things.
According to Buddhist theory, one's physical eyes may be opened, yet they
perceive only darkness, while with eyes closed, when one is engaged in
meditation, perfect spiritual insight is possible. To Hindus, the visible world
is an illusion (*maya*) which can be overcome by meditation upon the supreme.
The highest aim of the religious devotee, or *yogin*, is to "see" with his
spiritual eyes the eternal essence with which he tries to identify (*samadhi*).

> The seer sees not death,
> nor sickness, nor any distress.
> The seer sees only the All,
> Obtains the All entirely.[19]

The *ūrnā* of Hindu deities is believed to emit rays of light and even lightning.
There is a well-known story about Kama, the god of love, who disturbed
the meditation of the god Shiva by inspiring him with amorous thoughts about
his wife Parvati. The angered god thereupon burned Kama to ashes with
fire that flashes forth from his third eye.[20] Thus the *ūrnā* is not entirely
free from destructive associations, and, at least in the story, it recalls the
powers of the evil eye in Western art and mythology.

It should be noted that the meaning of the Sanskrit term *ūrnā* is not *sight*
(*caksus*) or eye (*aksha*) but "circle of hair between the eyebrows."[21] This
recalls the joined eyebrows of the eye idols of Brak and of most Mesopotamian
sculpture. Joined eyebrows are still found today among most Armenians
and Persians. The joined eyebrows of Mesopotamian art seem to be derived
from a racial characteristic of the Mesopotamian people. It is possible that
the *ūrnā* of Hindu and Buddhist divinities is nothing more than an adaptation
of the joined eyebrows found in the arts of the Euphrates-Tigris Valley which
diffused to the East, like certain other of its contributions, such as stamping
seals and the pottery wheel.

In conclusion, it may be stated that Western art used the exaggerated eye

8 Oriental Eyes. Gautama Buddha,
Japanese, c. XV to XVI Century A.D.
Courtesy of the A. K. Gordon
Collection, New York

8

whenever a heightened spiritual or emotional expression was demanded. As
Christianity preserved certain mystical concepts of the Ancient Near East, so did
its art. The strong oriental mysticism pervading Christian thinking was not
properly understood before the discovery of the Dead Sea Scrolls in 1947. These
documents, deposited in almost inaccessible caves near the Dead Sea by a
mystic sect of Judaism, the Essenes, are replete with concepts of Persian origin,
such as the opposition of the principle of light with the principle of darkness,
righteousness and evil, and matter and spirit. These ideas found their way
into the New Testament. There, too, is the eye as a symbol of life, intelligence,
and the soul: "The light of the body is the eye." (Matt. 6:22)

The inspiration of Christian art derives directly from the subject matter of the
Gospels as well as from their spirit. The Christian teachings aimed at a
spiritualization of all values: "Wherefore henceforth we know no man after the
flesh" (II Cor. 5:16). In other words, no man or woman was to be looked at
from the human (physical) point of view, but from the point of view of his
spiritual being. Though Christian art in general inherited three distinct stylistic
traditions—a Hellenistic one of suave body movement and classical compositional
schemes, a barbarian one of incredibly dynamic linear emphasis, and a
Byzantine-oriental one of exaggerated eyes and stereotyped frontal positions—
the Byzantine-oriental tradition had the most profound affinity with the Christian
mystical interpretation of life. The tendency to point beyond the physical
appearance directly to the soul was the mainspring of Byzantine art.

Hellenistic treatment of Christian subject matter derives from a non-
Christian world of thought. It was an attempt to achieve with naturalism what
Byzantine art actually achieved with abstraction and other oriental stylistic
and symbolic elements, namely, the destruction of the physical appearance

of the body in favor of the soul. The Hellenistic style, in spite of personalized facial expressions, symbolizes not the abiding world of the spirit (in the Christian sense) but fleeting moments of emotion dramatically represented. Only when the mystical orientation of the Gospels was no longer stressed, or when it was repudiated, as by the neopaganism of the Renaissance, did a body-centered style replace the soul-centered style of the Christian Orient. Due to copying, diffusion of manuscripts, and traveling artists, there were always pockets of Hellenism in both the early Christian and the Byzantine styles, but the oriental conventions were more naturally suited to express the Christian concept which Paul summed up in his Second Epistle to the Corinthians: "While we look not at the things which are seen, but at the things which are not seen: for the things which are seen *are* temporal; but the things which are not seen *are* eternal" (4:18).

A compromise between physical (Hellenistic) and spiritualized (Byzantine-oriental) emphasis in representing Christian subject matter can be detected in certain icons which portray sacred or imperial personages. In some the dominating figures are rendered in flat, dematerialized forms, they are frontal, and their wide-open, exaggerated eyes stare at the beholder; while the surrounding scenes are treated naturalistically, with three-dimensional draperies and well-carved floral motifs. Those elements of the icons which were to suggest spiritual awareness or a spiritual state of being were treated in an oriental manner, in which exaggerated eyes play such a prominent role, and the secondary, decorative elements were treated more naturalistically, in a Hellenistic manner.

It was the Byzantine-oriental rather than the Hellenistic tradition which radiated West and contributed to the formation of the Romanesque style. The typical intensity of Romanesque and Gothic saints is due in no small part to the attenuation with which eyes were carved, and the more exaggerated the eye, the more ecstatic the expression. The subordination of art to didactic purposes during the Middle Ages led to strong exaggeration, not only of the eyes, but also of gesture and posture.

Medieval art confirms the axiom that when a magic world view prevailed at a given period, eyes were exaggerated. The people were surrounded by the fantastic, the superstitious, and the miraculous. Legends of crying statues, healing images, and other miraculous properties of art were widespread. "The Church not only left room for many superstitions, but too often deliberately encouraged them. The sceptic on the one side, and the superstitious man on the other, took strength to themselves from the reckless way in which the clergy introduced the miraculous into ordinary life. Not only did they sometimes teach that sovereign virtues were inherent in mere attendance at their services, attentively or unattentively, and in the mere sight of such images as that of St. Christopher, but they endowed relics and pious gestures and exclamations with the same miraculous powers."[22] Of St. Suso it is related that one day he succeeded in curing a blind man by first rubbing his hands upon a wall on which were painted the figures of some holy Apostles and then touching the eyes of the sick person.[23] The chronicler Ekkehard even relates that one statue of St. Mary which the artist Tuotilo was executing at Metz was actually carved by the Blessed Mary herself.[24] The currents which created these legends also contributed to the exaggeration of the features of the face, for the artists existed and created in the same miraculous milieu.

As a result of the increasing acceptance of nature and the growing humanism of the late Gothic period, the treatment of eyes becomes more subdued. This also applies to the early Renaissance style with its concentration upon aesthetic rather than spiritual problems. Attention to the physical beauty of individuals did not permit exaggeration of the eye, for that would have destroyed the "dignity" and "harmony" which Leon Battista Alberti stressed in lieu of intensity of feeling and expression.[25] In his highly influential book *On Painting*, he advocates self-restraint and the avoidance of excess. But above all he prefers dignity and harmony of all parts; otherwise, the painting may show the too fiery and turbulent imagination of the artist.[26] That may be the reason that suffering saints in early Renaissance paintings, like St. Sebastian, always look dreamy and bored while arrows pierce their flesh. When spiritual intensity again became an issue, however, as it did during and after the Counter-Reformation, exaggeration of eyes, posture, and gesture inevitably return.

Modern art rediscovered the eye as a symbol of the soul. Since the late seventeenth century it had been all but forgotten, for the centuries of Reason and Enlightenment did not suffer a reminder of the spirit lurking within. Neoclassicists thought that the problems of man could be expressed with

9   René Magritte, The False Mirror
(1928). Courtesy The Museum of
Modern Art, New York

restraint, good manners, and reason; the Rococo preferred the exaggeration of details of the feminine body. They did not understand the powers of the eye because they did not understand themselves. They hid behind a veil of respectability as if the powers of the psyche did not exist.

Expressionism has seized upon the eye as a visual symbol of its mystical tendencies. The prevalence of primitive masks in Expressionist paintings (Ensor, Picasso, Nolde, Klee) is due to the fact that masks symbolize the alter-ego par excellence. They mock and shock yet suggest at the same time that behind their grin and their hollow eyes another, truer reality lies hidden. Van Gogh, Munch, Kirchner, Kokoschka, and many others painted eyes that search and stare. These intensified eyes, symbols of personal tragedy, project violently outward trying to discover meaning in a hostile cosmos.

Surrealism penetrated even deeper into the realm of the psyche. It explored the inner visions of the artist at the expense of the outer vision and thus discovered the landscape of the soul. As Chirico expressed it, "What I hear is worth nothing to me; there is only what my eyes see when they are open and more often when they are closed."[27] The emphasis in this statement is on the vision which the surrealist achieves with eyes turned inward, that is, closed. In this manner the artist can accept nature once more, but only on his own subjective terms.

When René Magritte painted his prophetic eye in the sky, clouds drifting through the iris, he closed the circle that began with prehistoric art. (Fig. 9) The eye of man was projected into the sky to become the eye of God, and man and God look at each other in astonishment, as it were, at their mutual discovery. Since it is the same eye, the soul of man merges with that of the cosmos. No one has summed up better the double meaning of the eye of God than the German mystic Meister Eckhardt. "The eye by which I see God is the same as the eye by which God sees me. My eye and God's eye are one and the same—one in seeing, one in knowing, and one in loving."[28]

The Smile of the Buddha

THE INFINITE SERENITY that pervades Buddhist religious images is due largely to the beatific smile playing around the corners of the mouth of most Buddhas and Bodhisattvas. (Fig. 10) The graceful pose of the feet, the sinuous curves of drapery and upper torso, are climaxed by a smile expressing indescribable bliss.

The recognition of feelings, emotions, and passions through outward signs and expressions (pathognomic), which have been studied in the West since Sir Charles Bell's *Essay on the Anatomy and Philosophy of Expression* (London, 1806), did not exist in ancient India. To Buddhist artists the smile was rather an allegory of the belief that death is release from *samsara*, the wheel of rebirth, and that *nirvana*, extinction, therefore, is bliss.[1] The smile entered Buddhist art relatively late in its history; it is necessary first, then, to investigate its origin and the reasons for its adoption.

The Great Enlightenment of the Buddha took place in *samadhi*, or complete absorption. This state of highest meditation was the aspiration not only of all Buddhists but of uncountable yogins before and after Buddha. *Samadhi is*

10

characterized by the stilling of all bodily senses as well as of all thoughts. It is a
temporary state of loss of self-consciousness, and the yogin who has achieved
this supreme feat of concentration no longer cares whether he smiles or not. As
long as a yogin is still conscious of his own smile, he has not achieved *samadhi*.
During the meditation that led to the Great Enlightenment, according to the
earliest sources, Buddha went through a series of trances. During the fourth
trance he rose beyond all those sensations, physical and mental, which could
produce a smile. "Abandoning pleasure and abandoning pain, even before
the disappearance of elation and depression, I attained an abode in the fourth
trance, which is without pain and pleasure, and with purity of mindfulness and
equanimity."[2] In the famous sermon to the Five Monks he stated, "the learned
noble disciple feels loathing for the body, for feeling, for perception, for the
aggregates, for consciousness. Feeling disgust he becomes free from passion,
through freedom from passion he is emancipated, and in the emancipated one
arises the knowledge of his emancipation . . . ."[3]

Similarly, the Dhammapada deprecates sensations that could lead to a smile. "The wise do not show variation (elation or depression), whether touched by happiness or else by sorrow. . . ." "If you make yourself still as a broken gong you have attained *nirvana*, for agitation is not known to you." "He who formerly was thoughtless and afterwards became reflective (sober) lights up this world like the moon when freed from a cloud." "From enjoyment arises grief, from enjoyment arises fear. To one who is free from enjoyment there is no grief. . . ." "Him I call a *brahmin* who like the moon is stainless, pure, serene, undisturbed, in whom joyance is extinguished."[4]

The ethos of primitive Buddhism precludes that expression which we recognize and describe as a smile. When the Dhammapada speaks of happiness and bliss (XV: 204), it is the happiness of *nirvana*—extinction of all physical, emotional, and mental sensations. The slow development of Mahayana metaphysics overshadowed the harshness of primitive, or Hinayana Buddhism, and it is significant that there were no anthropomorphic images of the Buddha until about the first century A.D. in the Gandhara School.[5] But even the rise of Mahayana doctrines does not satisfactorily explain the characteristic smile of the Buddha, for the first anthropomorphic images of Buddha were of the contemporary Gandhara School and were of sober and serious mien. (Fig. 11)

The smile is a universal symbol of love, recognition, and human communication in general. It is a basic axiom that children do not smile at birth, but that the smile develops between the first and third months as a response to social stimulation.[6] This refers, no doubt, to recognition of the mother, who cares for her child and who tries by various means to elicit a response. One pediatrician disregards all other stimuli, even the satisfaction after being fed. "The first smiles are always in response to social overture, when the mother talks to her baby. If the mother says . . . that the smiles were in response to other stimuli or not in response to any stimulus at all the story should be disregarded."[7]

One school of thought assigns social stimulation as the origin of the smile; another, satiation. Erasmus Darwin, as early as 1794, stated that the sphincter muscles of the mouth relax after the fatigue of sucking; this relaxation is visibly embodied in the infant's smile.[8] In "The Smiling Response," René Spitz and K. M. Wolf discuss its origin as follows: "The stimulus by which its [the baby's]

11 Buddha and Worshipers, Gandhara
(I–III Century A.D.). Hewitt Fund,
1913, Courtesy The Metropolitan
Museum of Art, New York

11

smiling can be consistently evoked must be a stimulus coming from a human partner. Various manifestations of the human partner can evoke a baby's smile. Referring to what we have said above about psychology being the science of human interrelations, it is of interest that smiling develops at a very early age into an essentially social manifestation, the manifestation of pleasure when beholding the presence of a human partner." Their summation is as follows: (1) The infant experiences its relationship with its mother emotionally. The infant responds with a smile to this experience. From the third to the sixth month the signal of this experience is a configurational stimulus originating within the human face. (2) Disturbances in the emotional relations between mother and baby inhibit the development of the smiling response. (3) Normalcy of the smiling response becomes, therefore, one of the criteria of normalcy of the emotional relation of the infant with its mother. (4) The human being establishes its first human relations with its mother. This first relation is the basis of, and determines the pattern for, all later social relations. Therefore, it may be a prognostic indicator of the infant's later capacity for social contact and social relations.[9] Social stimulation provokes a smile from without, physical satisfaction from within; both undoubtedly have a strong bearing upon the origin and significance of the human smile. With more mature children and with adults, smiling and laughter are closely related.[10]

Images of the Buddha do not stand or sit smiling blissfully or mysteriously as symbols of warm human relationship or of love; indeed, Gautama began his quest for the truth by abandoning his mother Maya, his father Suddhodana, his wife Yasodhara, and his son Rahula. The smile of the Buddha obviously cannot derive from such intensely human relations. But there are several other possibilities for the smile. There is the smile not only of the healthy and the loving, but also of the sick and the lonely. There are several styles of art with a definite smile, such as the Greek Archaic and Etruscan; and, finally, there is the smile of the dead. Whatever the source, there must be a compelling relationship between the smile and Buddhist teachings.

Although the smile as such is judged as a symbol of intelligence,[11] a fixed smile is a sign of vacuity. There are several disorders and conditions which produce a so-called smile—senility, aphasia, and others, such as cataplexy and

Huntington's chorea. A symptom of the latter disease is the contraction of the facial muscles resulting in a so-called smile combined with fatuous euphoria. Also, Wilson's disease (hepato-lenticular degeneration) produces spasms as well as a characteristic smile, in younger patients giving "a curious complacent aspect to the features. . . . some patients smile constantly."[12] Buddha, however, was a person of unusual intelligence and tremendous will power, as demonstrated by the years of yogic training before the discovery of the Four Noble Truths and the Eightfold Path.[13] He was familiar with Upanishadic, Brahminical, and yogic thought and used rigorous logic in many of his discourses. We reject, therefore, the smile of the disturbed, insane, and senile as a possible source for the smile of the Buddha, as sculptors conversant with Buddhist spiritual tradition would not have looked to this source for inspiration.

Superficially, the popular analogy between the Greek Archaic and the Buddhist smiles seems convincing, and some scholars have gone so far as to call the smile of the Buddha "archaic." It has long since been realized that the iconography of Gandhara Buddhas can be traced without difficulty to Greek and Roman prototypes in the typical stance, toga, gestures, slight twist of the body, standing and playing leg, etc.[14] It is important to note that Gandhara Buddhas from the first to the fourth century A.D. do not smile blissfully (Fig. 12). The Greek Archaic smile is a conventional expression with sharply outlined lips lifting up the corners of the mouth in either a strong curve or a "V" (Fig. 13). In some cases it borders on the grotesque, and, in fact, a strongly exaggerated archaic smile does appear on many archaic gorgons and grotesques.[15] The Greek Archaic smile does not suggest introversion or profound thought. It belongs to well-developed nude males stepping ahead with confidence and with heads erect, and represents physical rather than spiritual awareness. Most so-called archaic Apollos are *Kouroi* (youths), Olympic winners whose prowess was mainly physical.[16] In other words, these nude, healthy children of nature step forward, as it were, into life or toward other athletic contests. They convey the desire not to reject life, but to affirm and conquer it.

The Greek Archaic smile appears somewhat before the middle of the seventh century B.C. and vanishes approximately 480 B.C. with the beginning of the Transitional style. In the development of Greek sculpture the smile gives way,

12 Head of Buddha, Gandhara (I–III
    Century A.D.). Rogers Fund, 1913,
    Courtesy The Metropolitan Museum
    of Art, New York

13 Archaic Greek Head (2nd quarter, VI
    Century B.C.). Rogers Fund, 1921,
    Courtesy The Metropolitan Museum
    of Art, New York

12   13

with the emergence of the Classic style, to a serene, detached, almost stoic
expression. Toward the second half of the fourth century B.C., the faces of
Hellenistic sculptures achieve strong expressions reflecting a variety of
moods, but the sublime smile which we associate with certain styles of Buddhist
art is absent, particularly at the time of the first serious contacts between Greece
and India toward the end of the fourth century B.C. as a result of Alexander's
conquest. The Hellenistic style does not eschew introspection; the mood is
rather one of suffering and tragedy reflected in exaggerated gestures and facial
expressions.[17] Buddhist world rejection resulted not in such drama, pathos,
and exaggerated expressions and gestures, but in greater serenity and inwardness,
as if the only bliss that can be achieved amidst the insecurities of life lies in
the individual's withdrawal into himself.

   For the above reasons the Greek Archaic smile must also be rejected. In Greek
art the smile appears during the seventh century B.C. and later gives way to
serene or dramatic unsmiling expressions, while Buddhist art presents the first
Buddhas serene and sober and the typical smile enters later. Another reverse
process may be noted: The earliest Greek Archaic *Kouroi* are flat, patterned, and
ornamental; in time they relax to more and more fluid positions and forms. The
first Buddhist images of the Gandhara School are graceful in stance, with
standing and playing legs, some turns of body and head, flowing soft togas; they

develop into more and more stylized and stiff positions and forms. In other words, the first images of the Buddha are "classicistic" and later become stylized, or "archaistic," while Greek art begins, of course, "archaic" and subsequently develops the Transitional and Classic styles. Another argument is the time differential between the Greek Archaic and Buddhist smiles—over 800 years. No significant diffusion of art from West to East took place during the archaic Greek period. On the contrary, it has often been noted that there is rather an Egyptian and Assyrian influence radiating into Greek monumental sculpture. When Greek aesthetic conventions and techniques were finally diffused into North India, the Greeks themselves had either forgotten or rejected the smile as an expressive means.

The smile of the Buddha, then, does not derive from the normal smile of human beings, which is a sign of love, communication, and human relationship. Nor is it the smile of the sick and the insane. And any influence from Greek Archaic art has been dismissed. There remains one last possibility, the apparent smile of the dead, the *risus sardonicus*. There is, indeed, a remarkable connection between the smile of the dead and that of the Buddha who has "overcome life" and is "dead to life."

Buddhism has an awareness of the phenomenon of physical death, as does Hinduism, from which it sprang. Hinduism traditionally has had an extraordinary preoccupation with death and has worshiped it in the form of Kali, the fierce and black consort of Shiva who, in one of his aspects, is the cosmic destroyer. As far back as the Veda there is Yama, the Lord of Death, who "is still to some extent an object of terror."[18] The Upanishads declare death to be an illusion which can be overcome by correct knowledge. This did not, however, end the preoccupation with death; its denial did not wipe out the inevitable, but it did, at least, teach its acceptance.[19] Besides the well-known instances in the Upanishads which promise that knowledge will overcome death, there are others which face it more realistically:

> Verily, what those functions undertook of old even that they accomplish today. Therefore one should practice but one activity. He should breathe in and breathe out, wishing, "May not the evil one, Death, get me."

After death there is no consciousness!

As a heavily loaded cart goes creaking, just so this bodily self, mounted by the intelligent Self goes groaning when one is breathing one's last.[20]

In the great dialogue between Yama (death) and Naciketas, in the first chapter of the Katha Upanishad, Yama evades the searching questions about death which prove how aware the ancient Hindus were of this mystery:

NACIKETAS:

This doubt that there is in regard to a man deceased:
"He exists," say some; "He exists not," say others—
This would I know, instructed by thee!
Of the boons this is boon the third.

DEATH:

Even the gods had doubt to this of yore:
For truly, it is not easily to be understood.
Subtile in this manner (dharma).
Another boon, O Naciketas, choose!
Press me not! Give up this one for me!

·   ·   ·   ·   ·   ·   ·   ·   ·   ·   ·

DEATH:

. . . O Naciketas, question me not regarding
dying (maraṇa)![21]

Buddhists were, of course, aware of this tradition, and Yama, the ancient god of death, is mentioned in the Dhammapada. There the state of dying and death are acknowledged, somewhat wistfully, in two instances:

Some (who are not learned) do not know that we must all come to an end here; but those who know this, their dissensions cease at once by their knowledge (6).

Before long, alas, will this body lie on the earth, despised, bereft of consciousness, useless like a burnt faggot (41).

14 Head of a Youthful Buddha,
    Cambodia (XII Century A.D.). Rogers
    Fund, 1923, Courtesy The
    Metropolitan Museum of Art, New
    York

15 Death Mask, L'Inconnue de la Seine

14   15

Gautama Buddha did not come to teach men how to live more happily; he taught the Way of overcoming life. The most important tenet of Buddhism is expressed to artists and worshipers alike in an easily grasped, compelling manner —through the blissful smile. It is an idealized expression of the desire to die to the world and to enter upon the path of liberation which ends in *nirvana*.

Buddha's smile could have been inspired only by the observation of the apparently blissful smile of corpses, which was interpreted as a meaningful, almost intelligent reaction to death as a wonderful, desirable, and superior state of being, as the long tradition of Hindu and Buddhist thought implies. This smile, the so-called *risus sardonicus*, produced by a contraction of the facial muscles in rigor mortis, must have made a startling impression upon the prescientific minds of Hindus and Buddhists. It seemed proof that the dead had an experience that was pleasurable. It was this interpretation, or misinterpretation, that led to the smile in Buddhist art, the most exquisite allegory of death in the entire history of art. (Fig. 14)

That the *risus sardonicus* sometimes conveys the expression of indescribable bliss is illustrated by the well-known death mask of L'Inconnue de la Seine (Fig. 15). This unknown woman drowned herself in the Seine early in the twentieth century, and a sculptor who saw her body in the Paris morgue was so struck by her beauty that he cast her death mask.[22] The similarity to certain Buddhist images of the Wei period is striking (Fig. 10). The same ethereal smile suggests an experience of unearthly beauty. The smiling countenance in connection with death is also known in Etruscan art. There are several sarcophagi with banquet scenes of husband and wife in which smiles appear on the effigies of the dead. A well-known example is the terra cotta sarcophagus from Caere, c. sixth or fifth century B.C., now in the Villa Giulia in Rome (Fig. 16). The banquet scenes reinforced by the colorful frescoes in the tombs imply that the Etruscans hoped to continue in the after-life activities and pleasures which they enjoyed on earth. This is, of course, in direct contrast to the smiling Buddha. He sits or stands in solitary splendor, withdrawn, having finally overcome all expectations and desires of a future existence either on earth or in the beyond.

Having discussed the allegorical meaning of the smile of the Buddha, we can now turn to its morphology. A smile is the coordinated interplay of several muscles. In an explicit smile the angle of the mouth is drawn upward by the *zygomaticus* and backward by the *risorius*, which together retract the *anguli oris*, or corners of the mouth. This complex action also involves the *orbicularis oris*, or sphincter muscle, which surrounds the entire mouth. A smile affects the *buccinator*, or cheek, which pulls the mouth toward the ascending branch of the mandible, swelling it up like a contracted biceps. The *depressor anguli oris*, on the other hand, depresses the angle of the mouth, pulling down the *rima oris*, or partition between the lips, imparting a sober, sad, or angry expression.[23]

In Buddhist art there are five recognizable types of smiles: hidden, implicit, explicit, sublime, and stereotype.

The hidden smile appears in certain examples of the Gandhara School (Fig. 12). The mouth is relaxed with gently curving vermilion borders, or edges of the lips. The position of the mouth, in spite of the undulating *rima oris*, is horizontal. The *anguli oris* are drawn neither upward nor backward but are slightly deepened and, in some cases, drilled so as to cast a slight shadow. The *orbicularis oris* is indicated. The expression is mild and serene.

The implicit smile (Fig. 17) has a barely perceptible upward curve of the *rima oris*, but the *anguli oris* are much deeper so as to cast a strong shadow. The slightly protruding vermilion border of the upper lip has a tendency to curve upward and merge into the *buccinator* as a continuous form; the *orbicularis oris*, therefore, is understated. The content expression is similar to that of some Egyptian Eighteenth Dynasty portraits.

16 Etruscan Sarcophagus di Caere (VI
Century B.C.). Villa Giulia, Rome

17 Head of Buddha, Gandhara (I–II
Century A.D.). Rogers Fund, 1913,
Courtesy The Metropolitan
Museum of Art, New York

18 Head of Buddha, Mathura. (II
Century A.D.). Courtesy Museum of
Fine Arts, Boston. Arthur Mason
Knapp Fund

17   18

The explicit smile (Fig. 18) has the mouth slightly stretched backward and
upward. The *rima oris* curves up, noticeably contracting the *buccinator*. The
anguli oris are deeply carved, and the *orbicularis oris* is indicated. The expression
is one of satisfaction and happiness. This type of smile does not appear in
those Gandhara sculptures which are patterned after Graeco-Roman prototypes,
but it appears in examples from Mathura, which are based upon native Hindu
traditions, and continues into the Gupta style and even beyond into non-Buddhist
Hindu art.[24] The absence of the explicit smile in Gandhara scriptures is
demonstrated by the strong downward curve of the *rima oris*, which gives the
face a sober expression.[25] Some Gandhara carvings, however, have a serene,
pensive expression due to the wide open-eyes, as in certain bas reliefs in the
Peshawar Museum.[26] In other words, the first smiling Buddhas derived from
a Hindu tradition which employed the smile as an allegory of release (*moksa*)
and *nirvana*, two concepts entirely foreign to the Greek world view.

The sublime smile is the most inward and ecstatic smile in Buddhist art and is
characteristic of two styles: Wei (Fig. 10) and Cambodian art of about
the twelfth century A.D. (Fig. 14). In this type of smile the *rima oris* curves strongly
upward, the *anguli oris* are pulled upward and backward, and the *orbicularis
oris* is noticeable. The vermilion borders of Wei and Cambodian sculptures are
strongly delineated. The *buccinator*, particularly in Wei sculptures, is
contracted and rather heavy. It is not as prominent, although it is noticeable, in

19 Head of a Bodhisattva, Gupta (V–VI Century A.D.). Rogers Fund, 1933, Courtesy The Metropolitan Museum of Art, New York

20 Head of Buddha, Sung Dynasty (960–1279 A.D.). Iron. Fletcher Fund, 1961, Courtesy The Metropolitan Museum of Art, New York

19   20

Cambodian carvings, where the lips tend to flatten, if not stretch. The expression of sublimity is enhanced by the squinting eyes, as well as by the raised eyebrows, of Wei sculptures, and by the closed eyes of Cambodian images.

The stereotype smile (Fig. 19) is indicated by the marked upward curve of the *rima oris*, bordering on a smirk in certain examples. It seems frozen and perfunctory. Often the *rima oris* is V-shaped or parted. It is the result of repetition by rote. The stereotype smile, U- or V-shaped, appears early in some examples of the Gupta style and becomes a characteristic of most Buddhist styles after the explicit or sublime stage has been achieved. With exceptions, the smile becomes slightly stereotyped in India with the Gupta style, but it becomes entirely frozen in the Pala and later styles. It becomes stereotyped in Thailand after the thirteenth Century and in China with the Tang Period. In Japanese Buddhist art the sublime smile is not known; the implicit and hidden smiles and sober expressions appear at random. The stereotype-sober expression is a variation which occurs intermittently in the arts of China and Japan. (Fig. 20)

There is one stylistic phenomenon noticeable in most oriental national styles—namely, the gradual appearance of the smile and its development via a short implicit, explicit, and/or sublime phase into the stereotype smile. The explicit and later types of smiles always indicate a postarchaic phase, chronologically speaking. The archaic phase is characterized by the absence of the smile or, at most, by a hidden or implicit one. In the five types of smiles in Buddhist art we note first a gradual deepening of the *anguli oris* and, second, an increasing upward curvature of the *rima oris* until it becomes U- or V-shaped; finally the smile loses its expressive quality altogether.

In view of the fact that Gautama Buddha discovered that life is suffering, a discovery which culminated in the Four Noble Truths, it is remarkable to find the founder of Buddhism traditionally represented as smiling instead of with a tragic or serious expression, reflecting Plato's observation that "a man must be serious with the serious."[27]

Allegories of the Gothic Cathedral

THE MEDIEVAL CATHEDRAL is a link to a way of thinking now almost lost—a magical interpretation of the cosmos. It was the result of highly sophisticated building techniques in the service of mysticism and of scientific observation of nature in the service of a visionary image of the future. The cathedral is the only manifestation of the medieval creative genius in which all of its contradictions are reconciled, the spiritual and the material, the natural and the grotesque, science and magic, devotion to Christ and devotion to the Virgin Mary. The medieval concept of the cosmos, with its vast hierarchies, from the demonic to the celestial, was too much for the mind to contain—the cathedral alone symbolized them on a scale which the eye and the mind could encompass.

The recent flurry of important interpretive studies of the Gothic and its antecedents indicates the continued search for the deeper motivations of this style.[1] Definitive interpretations are neither possible nor desirable, for the subject of the cathedral is so complex, the differences between individual structures so varied, the technical means so daring, and its allegorism so complicated, that all one may hope is to penetrate deeper into its mysteries.

After Viollet-Le-Duc's monumental *Dictionnaire Raisonné de l'Architecture Française du XIe au XVIe siècle* (1863), there was a wave of rationalist criticism of Gothic architecture which only lately has lost ground to a more synthetic, interpretive approach. Leading allegorists of the Middle Ages, like William Durandus and even, to a certain extent, Abbot Suger, the guiding spirit of the Abbey church of St. Denis, took function for granted and saw only the symbolic meaning of form. Purely technical problems, such as the evolution of ribbed vaults and flying buttresses, do not illuminate the scope of the cathedral, which in one respect can be traced to the foundations of Christianity and beyond, and in another to a curious blending of mysticism and natural science of which it is such an outstanding expression. Although mysticism and science may seem strange bedfellows in our age of compartmentalization, during the Middle Ages there were many thinkers who saw no contradiction between the two. Hugh of St. Victor was a famous mystic noted for his classification of the sciences, and Albertus Magnus, even though a keen student of nature, yet believed that all inferior matter was imbued with "occult virtues" derived from the stars. The same is true of St. Hildegarde of Bingen, who wrote of religious visions as well as of plants, stones, trees, fish, birds, animals, reptiles, and metals in her compendious work *Medicinal Simples*. "A notable thing about even her religious visions is the essential conformity of their cosmology and physiology to the then prevalent theories of natural science."[2]

The development of Romanesque and Gothic cathedrals did not depend solely on ritualistic, social, and technical factors. While these, indeed, contributed in combination with other factors, such as the Roman basilica on the historical level and allegorism on the spiritual, the vertical accent and certain features of exterior and interior organization were inspired by nature. During the twelfth century there was a fortuitous conjunction of building techniques and scientific nature study which enabled the builders to incorporate adequately the allegory of the cathedral.

The allegorism of the medieval cathedral, its spiritual *raison d'être*, was inspired principally by Chapter 21 of the Revelation of St. John, who "saw the holy city, new Jerusalem, coming down out of heaven from God. . . ." The first

five verses of this chapter were customarily read at medieval dedication rites.[3]
Some scholars have gone beyond this description of the symbolism of the
cathedral, as did also many medieval theologians who were inspired by new modes
of devotion rather than by this scriptural tradition. Others have tried to
allegorize the cathedral in scriptural terms using sources other than Chapter 21
of Revelation. This is defensible insofar as it harmonizes with this chapter;
that is to say, the biblical sources and interpretations must agree with rather
than contradict each other.

The fundamental rule in an allegorical interpretation of sacred architecture is
that form follows not function but symbol. If the vision of the new
Jerusalem underlies the symbolism of the cathedral, the references in Chapter 21
of Revelation must be taken in their entirety, since the allegory is not quoted
out of context. This critical chapter contains several keys to details that are still
problematic. It discusses the new Jerusalem in many of its aspects, exterior as
well as interior. John's description, which has a bearing upon architecture, consists
of three parts: 1) the new Jerusalem descending to earth (1–3), 2) its architectural
description (9–21), and 3) the description of the interior of the new Jerusalem
(22–27).

The idea of the cathedral as a sacred city, a holy mountain, and the center of
the earth derives from the Hebrews and, through them, from the religious
traditions of the Ancient Near East, where the symbolism of the mountain of
God (*ziggurat*) was first conceived.[4] Every cathedral, like the temple at
Jerusalem, stands upon a "holy mountain" (Ps. 48:2). It is symbolically the
"center of the nations, with countries round about" (Ezek. 5:5). From it the
truth radiates in every direction, and around it, as around a cosmic axis,
everything revolves; thus every cathedral signifies both the physical and spiritual
center of the world.[5] It is built upon the "rock of salvation" (Ps. 95:1; I Cor.
10:4), upon the mountain on which God met his people (Exod. 19:11). The steps
which lead into the cathedral force one to ascend, as on the holy mountain
itself, so that man may see the face of God again.

Consistent with John's vision that the new Jerusalem is neither a single structure
nor a temple, but rather a magic city which descends upon a magic mountain,
Zion, the three zones in which the cathedral's exterior is articulated—1)

foundation, steps, and base; 2) aisle and nave elevation; 3) roof, towers, and spires—need not be interpreted too literally, for the entire exterior facade symbolizes the magic city and the magic mountain at the same time. This harmonizes with certain Old Testament prophecies which were fulfilled, according to the New Testament, during Christ's lifetime (". . . that what was spoken by the prophet Isaiah might be fulfilled" [Matt. 4:14]). A significant elucidation of John's vision is contained in a prophecy by Isaiah, who employed the terms "mountain" and "house of the LORD" synonymously: "It shall come to pass in the latter days that the mountain of the house of the LORD shall be established as the highest of the mountains, and shall be raised above the hills; and all the nations shall flow to it. . . ."(2:2). A cathedral, therefore, can never be high or fantastic enough, for it does not reflect any earthly city but recalls mountains of an unearthly landscape, with its crystalline structure and vertical accents, shadow-casting crevices and overhangs, steep slopes and tall needles.

An increasing desire for height, together with the expanding ground plan which became so typical of the Gothic cathedral, besides answering practical needs such as accommodating greater numbers of worshipers in the nave, more clergy in the rituals, and more relics in the side chapels, reflects a certain topographical awareness, at least on the exterior. In order to erect architectural magic mountains, the builders and ecclesiastics studied real mountains.[6] The exterior of the cathedral conforms to natural rock formations to an astonishing degree. The medieval mind, however, stood in superstitious awe of these mountains. In other words, architectural needs, nature study, and the miraculous entered into a strange relationship in the building of the great cathedrals.

The master builders and their learned ecclesiastical patrons drew their topographical and geological knowledge from two sources, popular and scientific. Popular knowledge of the world was disseminated by pilgrims and crusaders. The pilgrims had a decisive influence upon the growth of cathedrals; although this is universally acknowledged, it has been understood to apply to interior expansion due to relic worship. However, the pilgrims probably had as much to do with the exterior organization of the facades. Their romantic accounts by word of mouth and by letter of strenuous and often dangerous travel to centers of pilgrimages deeply affected the imagination of their contemporaries. Their more or less embellished stories laid the foundations for descriptive geology in that the people became aware of the topographical and geological features of Europe and the Near East.[7]

Among the favored centers of pilgrimage, besides Jerusalem, were the tombs of the apostles at Rome, the Shrine of St. James at Santiago de Compostella, the miraculous statue of the Blessed Virgin at Einsiedeln, and Monserrat, which was dedicated to the Virgin. The routes to these popular shrines led over steep mountains—the Alps or Dolomites (Italian shrines), the Swiss mountains (Einsiedeln), and the Pyrenees (Santiago and Monserrat). The awe-inspiring quality of these mountain chains, with their grouped peaks, high passes, sheer drops, tall needles, snow-covered summits, fantastic snowdrifts, and other features, made unforgettable impressions. Mountain climbing, too, though not widely practiced, attracted some intrepid souls. As early as 1188, John de Bremble, an English monk, ascended the great St. Bernard. In a letter to his subprior Geoffrey of Christ Church, Canterbury, he wrote: "I have been on the Mount of Jove; on the one hand looking up to the heaven of mountains, on the other shuddering at the hell of the valleys, feeling myself so much nearer heaven that I was sure that my prayer would be heard. 'Lord,' I said, 'restore me to my brethren, that I may tell them that they come not to this place of torment.' "[8] In 1250, King Peter III of Aragon climbed Mount Rochemelon, reporting that he had sighted a ferocious dragon upon it.[9] In 1307, a party of six clergymen climbed the Swiss peak Mons Fractus (or Pilatus); in doing so they defied the local ecclesiastical government and were jailed for the offense.[10] They probably received this opprobrium because at that time most people still believed that mountain tops were inhabited by dragons and evil spirits and were frequented by witches.

After the tenth century the people of northern Europe broke through the physical isolation which followed the breakdown of the Roman Empire's far-flung lines of communication. Through the pilgrims, crusaders, relic-vendors, traders, and wandering scholars they became aware of the topography of their world. This awareness was extended to nature in general, and we find natural plant forms in capitals, moldings, and decorations in most Gothic cathedrals. C. R. Morey noted that "it was the insistent Gothic quest of the concrete that led it into the most surprising phenomenon of mediaeval art—the shift to natural ornament."[11] This is not surprising at all if one considers the fact that nothing is as conducive to an appreciation of nature as traveling, particularly under the circumstances of the Middle Ages, when most travel was on foot or on horseback. In addition, abbots and monks often traveled on ecclesiastical business from monastery to monastery, and higher members of the clergy went as far as Rome. John of Salisbury, Bishop of Chartres, who went from England to France to study with Abelard, crossed the Alps ten times (!), journeyed twice from England to Apulia, and often traveled about France and his native land.[12] Between 1100 and 1250, seven emperors and their armies made no less than 39 journeys over Alpine passes. Of these imperial crossings nearly half were made by the Brenner, four by the great St. Bernard, six by the Septimer, three by Mount Cenis, two by the Lukmanier, and six by other passes.[13] Master builders and journeymen, as a rule, went from fabric to fabric, seeking employment in distant cities and countries. On building sites from England to Spain and Italy one could usually find quite a few foreign craftsmen working with native labor. Abbot Suger reports that on the rebuilding of the abbey church of St. Denis, during the first half of the twelfth century, "barbarian artists" were employed who were "even more lavish than ours."[14] In short, the stage was set for an exchange of information of different kinds, including technical know-how, stylistic features, observations of nature, and unusual topographical features gathered along the way.

Topography and geology were studied assiduously on a scientific level, particularly after the observations of Mohammedan scholars became available in Latin translations. Pliny's *Natural History* had given the medieval scholars their foundation in geology. His facts and fancies served until the vast reservoir of Mohammedan scholarship was tapped. Avicenna's work *De Mineralibus*, translated by Alfred of Sarashel, and the pseudo-Aristotle's *De Proprietatibus Elementorum*, translated from the Arabic by Gerard of Cremona in twelfth-century Spain, opened wide the floodgates of the increasing desire for scientific observations of the topography of the earth. Erosion of the earth and mountains by water was known to late Greek commentators, such as Alexander of Aphrodisias and Avicenna, the Mohammedan forerunner of St. Thomas, who accepted this "neptunic" theory but added his own so-called "plutonic" theory, that mountains were raised by eruptions due to earthquakes.[15] Avicenna also correctly understood how stalactites and stalagmites were formed.

Albertus Magnus wrote his systematic book on geology, *De Mineralibus et Rebus Metallicis*, based upon his Arabic predecessors, about 1260. Though he added some original observations, he accepted the then universally current theory of the magic properties of stones—the theory that underlies the desire of so many ecclesiastics for columns made of exotic and rare marbles for their cathedrals and precious stones for altars and ritual objects. Abbot Suger himself believed in the occult virtues of precious stones and proudly enumerated those adorning the main altar of St. Denis.

> *Often we contemplate, out of sheer affection for the church our mother, these different ornaments both new and old; and when we behold how that wonderful cross of St. Eloy—together with the smaller ones—and that incomparable ornament commonly called 'the Crest' are placed upon the golden altar, then I say, sighing deeply in my heart:* Every precious stone was thy covering, the sardius, the topaz, and the jasper, the chrysolite, and the onyx, and the beryl, the sapphire, and the carbuncle, and the emerald. *To those who know the properties of precious stones it becomes evident, to their utter astonishment, that none is absent from the number of these (with the only exception of the carbuncle), but that they abound most copiously.*[16]

A thirteenth-century scientific encyclopedia, *Speculum Regale*, contains detailed descriptions of glaciers, icebergs, geysers, and other natural phenomena. In Italy, Albertus Magnus' work held sway, though in the thirteenth centry Ristolo d'Arezzo made a number of interesting observations of the Appennines, describing the eroded castellated strata containing iron which lay over aqueous deposits of softer sandstones, shales, and conglomerates.[17] Bartholomew of England, a thirteenth-century Franciscan, in his *Proprietatibus Rerum*, devotes the fourteenth book to geology, defining mountains, hills, valleys, plains, fields, meadows, deserts, caves, and ditches. He describes over thirty particular peaks or mountain ranges, most of which are named in the Bible, such as Ararat, Bethel,

Hermon, Hebron, and Horeb. In the case of new localities and names for which he can find no ancient or early medieval authorities, he describes the province intelligently and accurately as it was in his own time. He praised such details as the stone and cement around Paris which gave it an advantage over other localities for building construction.[18]

In spite of the excellent observations and descriptions of nature by scholars like Albertus Magnus and Roger Bacon, the science of geology was not free of the miraculous. Thus one may find a perfectly scientific description of a natural phenomenon with its cause assigned to supernatural powers. An important element in the interpretation of the cathedral, therefore, is that the very stones of which it is constructed were believed to have "occult virtues." Abbot Suger in the above-quoted paragraph refers to "those who know the properties of precious stones," that is, their magical properties; one may be sure that most schoolmen were convinced that stones, and plants and animals as well, had these properties.

Albertus Magnus grants that the wonders worked by means of stones seem "more prodigious and marvellous" than those produced by simple substances, that the physical constitution of stones does not seem to justify the existence of such powers in them, and that "the cause of the virtue of stones is indeed occult." But he maintains that such occult virtues are well established by experience, "since we see the magnet attract iron and the adamant restrict that virtue in the magnet." He also claims to have seen a sapphire which removed ulcers.[19] He twice mentions that the "prodigious and marvellous" power of stones cannot really be understood without a knowledge of the three other sciences—magic, necromancy, and astrology.[20]

Grosseteste accepted Albertus Magnus' explanation of the marvelous virtues of gems as due to celestial influence, as did Vincent of Beauvais. "All things which are renewed in the inferior world, except such as are caused by the superior form of our reason, have their efficient causes in the inalterable and incorruptible superior world."[21] Although Albertus takes great pains to deny that the stars affect the free will of men, quoting Ptolemy of Lucca to the effect that the wise man rules the stars, he insists that they, in truth, are rulers of the world in those things which are subject to the world, namely things corporeal.[22]

There is little doubt that during the entire Middle Ages there existed the belief in a distinct relationship between stones and stars or, to put it more simply, between building materials and magic. This confirms the dictum of C. H. Haskins: "In the medieval mind the science of magic lay close to the magic of science."[23]

The well-known argument that natural plant forms which were used as decorative elements in the Gothic cathedral denote a "love of nature" (Emile Mâle and his followers) may not be as innocent as has been supposed. According to Albertus Magnus, the properties of plants are produced by the interaction of five virtues, of which the influence of the stars is predominant. "Its specific form, upon which its occult virtues largely depend, is given to the plant by the motion of the heavens, especially by the movement of the planets through the circle of the zodiac, and their position in relation to the fixed stars. Plants receive this influence at the time of their formation, when vapors, potentially seminal and formative, ascend from the depths of the earth and meet the dewy air as it ascends."[24]

Thus, before discussing technical problems or the symbolism of the exterior and interior of any cathedral, one should understand the extent to which the magic interpretation of the cosmos affected every part from the simplest building material to the most precious, every carving of plant motif, the colors of stained glass windows, symbols, ritual vessels—in short, every detail, material and symbolic, of the total fabric. In this connection it is interesting that Albertus Magnus believed that even art was under the influence of the stars. He asserted that a fundamental principle of this science (astrology) is that all things made by nature are moved first by celestial powers. He believed that it is the influence of the stars which incites the artist to create.[25] This throws an additional light upon the designing of the cathedral and its consecration. Guido Bonatti (thirteenth century), author of the *Liber Astronomicus*, goes so far as to give instructions for choosing a favorable hour for the building of churches, castles, and cities. His book was "intended for the use of Christians and the clergy."[26]

Some of this widespread knowledge was used in the exterior organization of the cathedral, for it enabled the master builders to express more "naturalistically" in architectural terms John's vision of the new Jerusalem descending to earth and Isaiah's prophecy that "the mountain of the house of the LORD shall be established as the highest of the mountains." The analogy between the church edifice and the mountain of God was made by Eusebius as early as the fourth century, thus establishing the precedent for this interpretation about 800 years before the Gothic style in which the allegory comes to full architectural expression. "To which city since the all-gracious God hath gathered us, through the grace of His Only-begotten, let each of the guests sing, yea all but shout, and say 'I was glad when they said unto me, we will go unto the house of the Lord'; and 'Lord, I have loved the beauty of thy house, and the place where thy glory dwelleth.' And let not only each one by himself, but also all together with one spirit and one soul, give honor and praise, saying: 'Great is the Lord, and highly to be praised, in the city of our God, in his holy mountain.' "[27]

Cathedrals located on the plains, from which they rise suddenly beyond the realm of man, express most effectively the concept of the magic city upon the magic mountain. In order to emphasize the cathedral's dominating mountainous impression, ecclesiastics, well aware of the allegorical meaning of their cathedrals, enforced the law that no secular building may rise higher than the parapet of the cathedral. "The Archbishop of Reims took delight in climbing to the eaves of his cathedral to sweep the surrounding town with a glass, with dire penalties for the owner of any man-made structure which projected above the level of the cathedral parapet."[28] Where cathedrals are located in hilly or mountainous regions, they blend naturally into the topography of the landscape. Cathedrals are as impressive near as from afar. Their sharp, asymmetrical silhouettes and deep indentations suggest not only individual mountains, as in Chartres, Paris, Amiens, Rheims, and others, but, as in the case of the Cathedral of Milan, a whole mountain chain. The Duomo of Milan is a veritable massif whose two thousand pinnacles and sculptures mirror the rugged outlines of the Italian mountains in the shadow of which it was built.

The typical Gothic cathedral "rises" like a mountain, from the east to the west, toward the tall towers as toward a peak. When seen from the east, there is a buildup of mass and volume—from the apsidioles, to the apse and apse roof, to the summit of the nave roof, to the flêche or to the western towers— suggesting a sequence of bulky masses which simulate groups of hills leading

up to a single or multiple peak. The western facade represents the sheer drop
or precipice of this magic mountain. Between the western towers (with or without
spires) there is a deep chasm through which the ridge of the summit with its
deep slopes is visible. A thirteenth-century cathedral with all its towers completed,
as in Viollet-Le-Duc's well-known sketch based upon the cathedral of Rheims, is
like a gigantic mountain with a main peak (the tower over the crossing) and
subsidiary peaks (the towers of the western facade and north and south transepts);
the spires are tall needles surrounding the ridge of the roof (summit). (Fig. 21)
The typical asymmetrical silhouette of the cathedral, with its towers rising
to different heights, reveals a spirit of capriciousness like that of nature, for
what natural peaks rise symmetrically?

From Nôtre Dame de Laon to Chartres, Amiens, and Rheims, and farther
to Strassburg and Cologne, an ever steeper drop of the western facade becomes
evident. The creviced surfaces of these cathedrals seem more eroded, too, as
if the builders had tried to anticipate the erosive hand of nature. Between pier
buttresses, vertical gulleys divide the surface, and the eye glides from fissure
to fissure, or furrow to furrow. Vertical colonnettes, like veins of harder material,
alternate with somewhat eroded, softer areas, creating crevices between them.
The flêche represents a rock tooth upon a ridge, and the transept becomes
a spur, one of the main ridges of the magic mountain. The western facade, or
precipice, is divided horizontally by moldings, which take the place of tiers of
ledges, outcroppings, and overhanging snow cornices, while flying buttresses
hang precariously like snow bridges and drifts from the cliffs of the nave elevation.

The purely functional purpose of single and multiple flying buttresses has been
greatly exaggerated. While lower buttresses, indeed, brace the nave walls and
dissipate vault thrusts to an extent, upper flying buttresses are wind braces,
according to John F. Fitchen, III.[29] Professor Fitchen concedes, however, that the
steeper roofs themselves, with their greatly increased weight, tend to resist
lateral wind pressure and to rotate under wind action. "Actually, from the
standpoint of wind alone, it was advantageous for these high, steeply-pitched
roofs to be relatively heavy. For there is a definite relationship between the
height of an object of a given base and its weight, when it comes to its stability
in resisting the overturning action of wind."[30] As far as we know, no Gothic

21 Sketch of the Cathedral of Rheims.
Viollet-Le-Duc, *Dictionnaire Raisonné*

21

cathedral has collapsed from wind pressure. As in many other architectural details, symbolic significance was read into purpose until the purpose become obscured and symbolism or decorative effect became the sole consideration, as in the case of the highly elaborate English fan vaults. Flying buttresses were often placed on relatively low structures for reasons which were obviously other than functional, as on the polygonal chapter house of the Cathedral of Lincoln and on many towers. The English, on the whole, resisted flying buttresses and erected lofty structures without them, such as the rebuilt clerestory of Gloucester with its vast windows, the nave of Tewkesbury, and many others. "Frequently also late spires were connected with their corner pinnacles by ornamental flying buttresses. It is remarkable how unsuccessful almost all are."[31] At any rate, the proliferation of multiple flying buttresses owes as much to symbolic as to practical considerations. Mountain tops are generally whipped by high winds, which not only erode stone surfaces but carve strange snow and ice drifts. There seems to be a distinct visual relationship between the architectural magic mountain with its flying buttresses and real mountains with their fantastic snow and ice bridges. This interpretation does not deny the functional aspect of flying buttresses but extends it from brace to symbol.

Extremely "eroded" cathedral facades, such as Rouen, Tours, and Cologne, give the impression of being in the process of exfoliation, a flaking or weathering of the stone due to age. Stained glass windows set back into square fields or pointed arches do not reveal their colors from the exterior but act, rather, as a pattern and glistening texture, bringing to mind *verglas*, the thin coating of ice or snow upon rock. Smaller details, such as crockets, turrets, niches, finials, and so forth, complete the weather-beaten appearance, simulating a mountain carved by the wind and snow for thousands of years.

The crystalline, angular structure of the cathedral attempts to conform, as far as architectural necessity allows, to John's description of the exterior of the holy city, the new Jerusalem. "And in the Spirit [one of the seven angels] carried me away to a great, high mountain, and showed me the holy city Jerusalem coming down out of heaven from God, having the glory of God, its radiance like a most rare jewel, like a jasper, clear as crystal" (Rev. 21:10–11). He describes it further: "It had a great, high wall, with twelve gates, and at the gates twelve

angels, and on the gates the names of the twelve tribes of the sons of Israel
were inscribed; on the east three gates, on the north three gates, on the south
three gates, and on the west three gates. And the wall of the city had twelve
foundations, and on them the twelve names of the twelve apostles of the lamb"
(Rev. 21:12–13). John's visionary city has four sets of gates, but only three sets
of gates (porches) are possible on the cathedral—west, north, and south. The
eastern elevation contains the round or square apse behind the altar, and porches
there would disturb the sanctity of the ritual. But the archivolts of the splayed
entrances often have choirs of angels carved into them to convey John's "twelve
angels at the gates." The attempt to erect larger and larger cathedrals with
higher naves and taller towers surmounted by steeples may have been inspired
in part by John; he noted that in size the heavenly city was "twelve thousand
stadia, its length and breadth and height are equal . . . its walls a hundred and
forty-four cubits" (Rev. 21:15–17). He goes on to say that "the wall was built
of jasper, while the city was pure gold, clear as glass" (Rev. 21:18). This explains
the exterior crystalline appearance noted above, but the city itself, made of
"pure gold, clear as glass," inspired the luminous quality of the interior, for the
Gothic was the first architectural style in history which, indeed, had translucent
walls.

Other of John's remarks concern the substance of the new Jerusalem, that
it was adorned with every jewel: "the first was jasper, the second sapphire, the
third agate, the fourth emerald, the fifth onyx, the sixth carnelian, the seventh
chrysolite, the eighth beryl, the ninth topaz, the tenth chrysoprase, the eleventh
jacinth, the twelfth amethyst" (Rev 21:18–21). As we remember, Abbot
Suger encrusted the altar of St. Denis with seven of the twelve precious stones
mentioned by John. He added one new one, sardius, and made a point of the
fact that one, the carbuncle, was missing. Since neither the sardius nor the
carbuncle was mentioned by John, Suger undoubtedly had their magical properties
in mind. That the medieval mind conceived of the cathedral as a magic city built
of precious stones is proved by Suger's account of the laying of the foundation
for the enlarged abbey church of St. Denis: "The Most Serene King himself
stepped down [into the excavation] and with his own hands laid his [stone]. Also
we and many others, both abbots and monks, laid their stones. Certain persons

also [deposited] gems out of love and reverence for Jesus Christ, chanting: *Lapides preciosi omnes muri tui.*"[32]

The interpretation of the cathedral as a magic city upon a magic mountain also answers more satisfactorily the problem of gargoyles and grotesques upon the summit or roof. Most scholars have either studiously avoided the subject or dismissed it with pious generalities.[33] Sedlmayer characterized their region as the "Sphere of Hell" and remarked, in his rather inconclusive discussion on this subject, that "these zones of hell are as yet too little investigated."[34] These fantastic upright representations of evil (as well as some horizontal water spouts, which, though grotesque, fulfill a functional purpose) complete the symbolism of the exterior of the magic mountain.

Mountain tops were always believed to be dwelling places of good or evil spirits. A well-known instance of this belief was the Walpurgisnacht in the mountains in central Germany. There, on the Brocken, the highest peak, during the night between April 30 and May 1, witches and evil spirits, led by Satan, would congregate and engage in a wild orgy. This pre-Christian festival marking the beginning of summer was christianized by connecting the date to St. Walpurga, the eighth-century English missionary who went to Germany. "Some of the cultus with which she was formerly honored, including her attribute of corn, may possibly have been transferred to her from the old heathen goddess Walborg, or Mother Earth."[35] The similarity between the name of the heathen goddess Walborg and St. Walpurga is rather distinct. The latter, however, is considered a protectress against magic arts, which links her firmly to the pagan festival in a negative form. The sculptors who placed grotesque representations of evil around the summit of the cathedral perhaps took evil too literally. They based their inspiration not only upon persistent popular superstitions, but also upon the remarks about evil, Satan, and demons in the Old and New Testaments.

In the Old Testament, Satan is mentioned repeatedly as the tempter (Job 1 and 2) and the adversary of man (I Chron. 21:1; Zech. 3:1–2). Evil spirits torment those whom God abandons (I Sam. 16:14–16). In the New Testament the existence of Satan, demons, and evil in general is a persistent theme. Overcoming temptation by Satan is part of the process of salvation; indeed, Christ himself was tempted by him (Luke 4:1–13). The Lord's Prayer refers to the ever present dangers of evil: "And lead us not into temptation, but deliver us from evil" (Matt. 6:13). Evil is a power against which one must always be on one's guard. "Be sober, be watchful. Your adversary the devil prowls around like a roaring lion, seeking someone to devour" (I Pet. 5:8). In other words, "the whole world is in the power of the evil one" (I John 5:19).

Most schoolmen took for granted the existence of Satan, demons, and witches. Vincent of Beauvais believed that demons inhabited the lower and misty air.[36] This would suggest the eaves of the roof of the cathedral as their natural habitat. Other scholars and theologians believed in dragons, basilisks, and other imaginary animals associated with evil. Albertus Magnus, for instance, believed that the mere glance and hiss of the basilisk was fatal. Though the reptile's glance will kill as far as its vision extends, its hiss is fatal not as far as it can be heard, but only as far as it is propelled by the basilisk's breath.[37] Even Roger Bacon still believed in dragons and that the eating of their flesh prolongs life and inspires wisdom.[38]

The magical arts, so widely practiced, were believed to be ultimately the work of demons. Albertus Magnus and some other schoolmen distinguished between two varieties of magic, one natural and good and the other demoniacal and evil.[39] It would be stretching the point to assume that the gargoyles and occasional obscene exaggerations represent good, or white, magic.[40]

These grotesques were placed upon the summit of the cathedral not to protect it from evil but as a reminder of evil, for how can Christians combat evil with evil? In a famous instance, Christ ridiculed this idea with a parable. "How can Satan cast out Satan? If a kingdom is divided against itself, that kingdom cannot stand. And if a house is divided against itself, that house will not be able to stand. And if Satan has risen up against himself and is divided, he cannot stand but is coming to an end" (Mark 3:22–27). Do these images on cathedrals like Nôtre Dame of Paris, Rheims, and others illustrate Christ's parable that when evil rises against evil its end is near, or do they represent the cosmic battle in which evil will be defeated (Rev. 20:1–13)? Or do they illustrate the strong belief held during the Middle Ages that evil was still "prowling around," and that Satan and his horde convened upon mountain tops? The latter is consistent with the magic mountain, the medieval belief in demons, and the representation of evil not as defeated but as very much alive.

If the interpretation of the exterior of the cathedral thus far is correct, then its entrance and interior must in some way conform to this architectural allegory. Entrances to cathedrals are exceedingly small and narrow in proportion to the height and width of the facades. Deeply splayed entrances, with or without overhang, strongly suggest entrances to caves. In some cases, such as the west front of Amiens, the door (mouth of the cave) is hidden within a deeply eroded entrance covered with tracery like hanging icicles. The typical Romanesque Lombard porch has two lions supporting colonnettes and canopy (overhang) which, like guardian animals of old, protect the entrance into the sacred cave. Past the overhang and narrow entrance one steps into a vast, dim cave. The interior of the cathedral, on one symbolic level, is a cave, the tall compound piers and the thin shafts upon them simulating stalagmites and protuberances which grew upon them by slow accumulation. And below the nave floor are deeper hollows (*confessio, crypt, undercroft*), which suggest a network of interconnecting caves.

John describes the interior of the New Jerusalem as follows: "And I saw no temple in the city, for its temple is the Lord God the Almighty and the Lamb" (Rev. 21:22). Since John states explicitly that he did not see a physical structure in the new Jerusalem, but the Lord as temple, the interior of the magic city should be interpreted in anthropomorphic terms.

Such interpretations of sacred architecture go back to Vitruvius. In his celebrated opening of Book III, he bases the proportions of the temple upon the measurements of the human body. "For without symmetry and proportion no temple can have a regular plan; that is, it must have an exact proportion worked out after the fashion of the members of a finely shaped body." In another place (Book I:2) he writes that "decor obeys conventions, that is, different orders will be suited best for various gods such as the Doric for Minerva, Mars, and Hercules, the Corinthian for Venus, Flora, and Proserpine, while the Ionic serves best Juno, Diana, and Bacchus." Vitruvius must have been familiar with the Stoic concept of the microcosm reflecting the macrocosm. Although his ideas did not become popular until the Renaissance, copies of his books were extant and were consulted during the Middle Ages.

When Vitruvius derived the proportions of the temple from those of a "finely shaped body," he did not have a female body in mind. Renaissance artists and architects, such as Francesco di Georgio, Pietro Cataneo, Cesariano, Leonardo, and

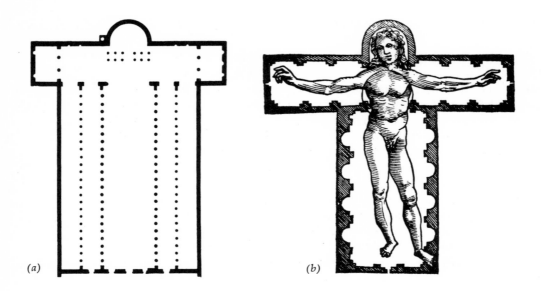

(a)   (b)

others, interpreting Vitruvius, applied their proportional schemes, so-called Vitruvian figures, to male bodies only. Pietro Cataneo even drew a nude male body within the confines of a basilica based upon a Tau cross plan. (Fig. 22b)

Christ compared his body to a temple, as is evident from the disputation recorded in John 2:18–21. "Destroy this temple and in three days I will raise it up. The Jews then said, 'It has taken forty-six years to build this temple, and you will raise it up in three days?' But he spoke of the temple of his body." Peter referred to him as "living stone" (I Pet. 2:4) and Paul following through this architectural imagery, compared the faithful to temples (I Cor. 3:16–17), buildings (I Cor. 3:9), and houses (II Cor. 5:1). The stones of which the cathedral is constructed symbolize Christ. "The very stone which the builders rejected has become the head of the corner" (Mark 12:10). He is the foundation (I Cor. 3:11) and the chief cornerstone in whom the whole structure is joined together (Eph. 2:20–21). The term "structure" is used here in the sense of the congregation of the faithful, but it can be applied to the physical structure in which the faithful become "united to the Lord . . . one spirit with him" (I Cor. 6:17). With this concept two fundamental

22 (a) Ground Plan of Old St. Peter's,
Rome (b) Pietro Cataneo, Vitruvian
Figure. *I Quattro Primi Libri di
Architectura*, Venezia, 1554

symbols coalesce into one—the interior of the cathedral, or temple, as the body
of Christ, and the body of Christ as a temple.

The Logos became incarnate in a male, Jesus. In the gospels it is his body that
is compared to a temple, living stone, foundation, cornerstone, and door. The
thirteenth-century allegorist William Durandus, basing himself upon such
scriptural precedence, interpreted the cathedral of his time anthropomorphically.
"The arrangement of a material church resembleth that of the human body: the
chancel, or place where the altar is, representeth the head: the transepts, the hands
and arms, and the remainder—towards the west—the rest of the body." He also
included the cruciform ground plan in his allegoric interpretation. "But some
churches are built in the shape of a cross, to signify, that we are crucified to the
world, and should tread in the steps of the Crucified."[41]

Christ's reference to himself as a temple must have impressed ecclesiastics and
builders long before Gothic cathedrals were erected. In other words, the well-
known argument that the cross plan as a symbol of the crucified applies only to
structures erected after about 1000 can no longer be defended. The cruciform plan
of most Western churches and cathedrals can be traced to Old St. Peter's in Rome
(326 A.D.). As one scholar has put it, "The whole solution at Old St. Peter's was
so masterly that it has been repeated with variations in every subsequent age down
to the present, and it is correct to say that this design, where Christian architecture
was first declared to the world, was the most influential church design ever
composed."[42] (Fig. 22a)

During the 4th century, which witnessed a new, tolerant attitude towards
Christianity (Council of Milan), the cross was being openly interpreted as a

symbol of victory. About this time, also, there emerged the interpretation of the cruciform basilica as a symbol of Christ. "St. Ambrose in 382 was among the first to emphasize that the cross plan of the Church of the Holy Apostles at Milan, which he laid out, was meant to symbolize the victory of Christ and of His cross."[43] This applied, no doubt, to Old St. Peter's and to other contemporary churches. "Yet it does not matter greatly which particular cross shape was meant, whether basilica plan in the shape of the Latin *crux capitata* as at Déas; whether it was the pattern of the T cross as at Bamberg or whether a Greek cross plan was referred to as in Arculph's description of the church at the well of Jacob. . . . The term [*similitudinem crucis; in modum crucis*] may possibly have been applied even to round edifices with cross chapels. . . . Occasionally the cross shape refers even to the pattern in which five churches are laid out with or around a city. . . ."[44]

Many other elements of the interior carry through this allegory of the body of Christ. Medieval ecclesiastics, intoxicated with allegorism, did not fail to appreciate the great possibilities of light as a symbol of the Incarnation. Light was not studied or understood as to its properties, but was thought of primarily in a mystical sense. It was believed to issue from the stars and to exert occult powers; in short, magical-mystical notions prevailed over scientific ones. Since the cathedral is primarily an allegory of John's vision, one must not overlook his and other scriptural references to light in favor of Neoplatonic light mysticism, which seems to be the tendency in recent scholarship. Durandus himself linked stained glass windows to the light of God. "The glass windows in a church are Holy Scriptures, which expel the wind and the rain, that is all things hurtful, but transmit the light of the true Sun, that is, God, into the hearts of the faithful."[45] While Neoplatonism, indeed, reinforced these notions, they were rooted in the scriptures which were studied no less on that account. What is more descriptive of the translucency of a Gothic cathedral than the words of Psalm 104:2, "[LORD] who coverest thyself with light as with a garment?" And when the Lord showed Zechariah the plan of the rebuilt Jerusalem, he said, "For I will be to her a wall of fire round about . . . and I will be the glory within her" (Zech. 2:5). The New Testament abounds with references to Christ as "the light of the world" (John 8:12), "the giver of light" (Eph. 5:14), "God is light" (I John 1:5), and so forth.

If the interior of the cathedral is anthropomorphic, then the stained glass windows are its "skin." They also symbolize various aspects of Christ's presence. Apse windows, like the star in the East, announce his birth (Matt. 2:2). They also represent "eyes," for the apse is the "head" of the cathedral: "his eyes were like a flame of fire . . . and his face was like the sun shining in full strength" (Rev. 1:14–16). The tall stained glass windows of the nave and aisles represent his "garment of light," for the body of the Lord is "covered with light." The rose in the western elevation represents the setting sun and announces his death, for after the crucifixion there was "darkness over the whole land" (Mark 15:33) or a solar eclipse (Luke 23:44–45). Under the western rose the tympanum of the central porch of many cathedrals contains scenes of the Last Judgment, that is, of death and resurrection. The rose window, in spite of its improbable name, is a symbol of the sun. It is either a lotus flower, a wheel, a star pattern, or a combination of these. "The Rosette—whether derived from the lotus or any other flower—forms an essentially solar symbol."[46] It is often placed in a dominating position in the western elevation symbolizing the setting sun, while the lights, small roses, and oculi in the eastern elevation represent the rising sun, or the morning star, another symbol of Christ. "I am the root and offspring of David, the bright morning star" (Rev. 22:16). As the lotus responds to heliotropism, turning its flower in the direction of the rising and setting sun, so the stained glass windows of the cathedral "turn" with the sun from the lights in the eastern apse to the rose in the western elevation. The worshiper responds to them in an analogous manner, not to the physical light, but, in a kind of spiritual heliotropism, to the "true light that enlightens every man" (John 1:9).

In most Gothic cathedrals there is no disposition made to admit the midday sun. In those cathedrals in which overhead lanterns are present, they only allow indirect light. This bears out the opinion of all mystics, including that of St. Bernard de Clairvaux, that the direct vision of God is a blinding experience. " 'That Vision which you asked to be shown is far beyond your powers, O my spouse,' says the Bridegroom, 'nor are you strong enough to look upon the marvellous light of midday wherein I dwell. . . .' "[47] The stained glass windows, as we have seen, may be considered the skin of the "body" of the cathedral; it follows, then, that the walls must be its flesh, and the ribs the bone structure. St. Bernard, in his *Commentary on the Song of Solomon*, compared Christ's flesh to a wall. "*Behold*

He standeth behind our wall, looking through the windows, looking through the lattices [I Cant. 2:9]. . . . The Bridegroom drew near the wall when He assumed flesh. The flesh is the wall. The taking of it unto Himself by the Bridegroom is the Incarnation of the Word. Moreover, the windows and the lattices through which He is said to look are, as I understand it, the bodily senses and the human affections through which He began to have experimental knowledge of all human needs."[48]

A major element of the Gothic interior is the ribbed vaulting, or the bone structure of the cathedral. The reason for the introduction of the ribbed vault is still unknown. Paul Frankl and many other leading scholars think that it was introduced mainly for aesthetic reasons: "the Gothic three-dimensional rib was used for the first time to substitute for and correct the shaky one-dimensional lines of the groins in Romanesque cross vaults. The rib first served the aesthetic function of satisfying the eye with the purity of the curve. Once it existed, it led not only to consequences in the realm of geometric construction, technical process, economy of material, statics and durability, but also in the realm of aesthetics and, in a narrower sense, of style."[49] Ribbed vaults precipitated a revolution in medieval architecture, for they enabled the builders to manipulate vast areas of space and light which are of the essence in Gothic architecture. The pointed ribbed vault, however, coincides with two remarkable developments in medieval life. The first, in the realm of religion, was the substantial increase of devotion to the Virgin Mary, and the second, in the realm of science, the dissemination of anatomical knowledge from the medical schools of Chartres, Salerno, Montpellier, and Bologna.

The extensive interest in human anatomy has not been adequately related to the development of the ribbed vaulting of Gothic cathedrals. Anatomical studies, particularly of the rib cage, helped the builders to clarify the allegory of the interior of the cathedral. These studies surely antedate the origin of the ribbed vault, and, while many points of contact between architecture and anatomy are still obscure, the anthropomorphic terminology of architectural members points to connections.[50]

In spite of alchemy and witchcraft, medicine was practiced throughout the Middle Ages. Most monasteries had infirmaries, and hospitals were founded by special orders of hospitallers like the Order of St. John of Jerusalem and the Brothers of the Holy Ghost. The latter founded their most renowned hospital as early as 1145 at Montpellier. When St. Bartholomew's hospital was founded in London in 1123, there were already eighteen others in existence in England. From the early thirteenth century, on the inspiration of Pope Innocent III, Holy Ghost hospitals were founded in almost every town in Christendom.[51] Peter Hispanus, who became Pope John XXI in 1276, wrote several works on medicine. Among the traditional treatments and superstitions which he repeated, there is also a long passage on the importance of the experimental method, or the "way of experience" coupled with "the path of reason."[52]

A revival of medical learning took place at Chartres as early as Carolingian times.[53] Theoretical anatomical studies were carried on through translations of medical works of the Persian Hali Abbas (d. 994) by Stephen of Antioch in 1127 and of the influential Canon of Avicenna by Gerald of Cremona, who also translated the anatomical works of the Persian Rhazes.[54] These works themselves depended on Arabic translations of Galen, the Roman medical genius of the second century.

The first medical school with a practical curriculum was located at Salerno in southern Italy. The regulations of Emperor Frederick II required that the medical student at Salerno take a course lasting five years which included anatomy and surgery. After passing an examination at the end of his course, he was required to intern for one year with a trained practitioner.[55] At the end of the twelfth century Salerno produced the first great Western surgeon, Roger of Salerno, whose book Practica Chirurgica was widely read.[56]

During the thirteenth century, when the Gothic reached its maturity, post-mortems were already being performed at the medical school of Bologna. The founders of its surgical school were Hugh of Lucca and his student, the cleric Theodoric Borgognomi. William of Saliceto, who taught at Bologna during that time, left a treatise on surgery which contains evidence of direct access to cadavers. Thaddeus of Florence openly practiced post-mortem examinations, as did his students. His most important pupil was the Norman Henri de Mondeville, who, after studying at Bologna, returned to France and lectured on anatomy at the medical school of Montpellier. An illustrated book of his on anatomy, intended primarily for his students at the school, nevertheless exerted great influence far beyond its walls.[57] The most eminent anatomist of the Middle Ages was Mondino de Luzzi (c. 1270–1326), who studied under Thaddeus of Florence at the same time as Henri de Mondeville. His *Anothomia*, written in 1316, is devoted entirely to anatomy. He practiced dissection and was a direct forerunner of the sixteenth-century anatomist Vesalius. The school of Bologna dominated anatomical studies until the sixteenth century, but its books and students strongly influenced the progress of anatomical studies beyond the Alps.[58]

In spite of the fact that cruciform cathedrals are primarily allegories of the crucified (St. Ambrose, Durandus), the great profusion of cathedrals dedicated to Nôtre Dame during the twelfth century and after was due to a shift in religious orientation and a corresponding reinterpretation of the interior of the cathedral in female terms. St. Bernard and many other mystics lavished their most abundant praise and adoration upon the Virgin. This devotion was shared by the sculptors who carved countless images of the Madonna and child. There is a tradition which likened her to a temple as early as St. Ambrose—she was not herself "a God in the temple" but "a temple for God."[59] This idea gained momentum after the Council of Ephesus in 431, when the *Theotokos* doctrine became dogma. Soon she was compared to a kingly castle, for she gave birth to a king, and to a "shining palace for the Lord of Eternity." She was the "wedding-chamber" where the Creator united himself with his creation, and she was likened to the "tent of the covenant into which God had entered to carry out the work of Atonement" and to the "Holy Tabernacle filled with the glory of God."[60] On occasion, the term *camera trinitatis* was employed, as was *domus*. To some mystics she was a throne when she held her divine son on her knee, as well as a vessel carrying a luck-bringing cargo.[61] Anselm of Canterbury called her the "Palace of universal propitiation . . . Vessel and Temple of the life and salvation of all. . . ."[62] And St. Francis of Assisi exclaimed, "Hail, palace of Christ, hail, tabernacle of Christ, hail, Mother of Christ!"[63] In short, there is a large body of devotional and mystical literature in which the Virgin Mary is compared to architectural structures. This imagery was applied to the Gothic cathedral and led to a growing ambivalence in its allegorism. Abbott Suger called the church edifice itself "our mother," although in another place he calls it the "house of God."[64] William Durandus, about a century later, manifested the same ambivalence when he wrote, "Again, the church is called the *Body of* Christ: sometimes a *virgin*, . . . sometimes a *bride* . . . sometimes a *mother* . . . sometimes a daughter. . . ." He described the edifice itself as "the proper spouse of Jesus Christ."[65]

This tendency led to a reinterpretation of important elements of the cathedral. The door, a favorite symbol of Christ, as we have seen before, became the virginal door of Mary, or the "Gate, through which has passed the king!"[66] This tradition survives even today. Of medieval porches dedicated to the Virgin, Damasus Winzen, paraphrasing Ezekiel 44:2, writes, "She is the door 'through which no man has passed.' "[67] The deeply splayed porches with their pointed arches certainly have anatomical connotations. In fact, the pointed arch was introduced in the West precisely when the worship of the Virgin Mary had reached popular proportions, and a new architectural style heralded the victory of a new direction in religious orientation.

The windows of the cathedral, which, according to Durandus, "transmit the light of the true Sun, that is, God," became symbols of Mary's virginity. A thirteenth-century Christmas carol, *Dies est laetitiae*, is an illustration of this.

> As the sunbeam through the glass
> Passeth but not staineth,
> So the Virgin as she was
> Virgin still remaineth.[68]

There is a literal translation of this concept in the famous Merode Altarpiece by Robert Campin. The central panel of this triptych, now at the Cloisters, Metropolitan Museum of Art, depicts the Virgin and the Angel of the Annunciation in her chamber. Through one of the two round windows behind the angel, light streams into the interior; there are seven rays, symbolizing the seven gifts of the Holy Ghost. Campin substituted these seven rays for the dove, the more conventional symbol of the Holy Ghost in most Annunciation scenes. The painter was familiar with the concept that Gothic stained glass windows symbolized the virginity of Mary, for he depicted Christ as a tiny infant, face down amidst the light rays, floating through the window into her chamber, carrying a miniature cross on his right shoulder.[69] In prayers in which the pious invoked the Virgin for the safety of their souls, she was often addressed as *Fenestra Coeli*, window of heaven.[70] Splayed porches and deep, pointed embrasures of windows undoubtedly lent themselves to being interpreted in female anatomical terms, and their suggestiveness became overwhelming (Fig. 23). At the same time, theologians were preoccupied with debating and defining the state of Mary's womb before, during, and after parturition.[71]

Most of the large Gothic cathedrals are built upon the cruciform ground plan, and at consecration rituals the verses from Revelation 21:1–5 were read. Was the primary masculine interpretation of the interior obscured by a secondary female one, or did it become esoteric as far as the laymen were concerned? A symbolic reinterpretation of architectural elements of the cathedral took place; in other words, there was a merger between traditional (male) and new (female) allegories.

Medieval ecclesiastics and builders became conscious of human anatomy in the

wake of the widespread teaching and practice of various medical schools in Italy and France, as noted above, and they used that knowledge to express the concept of the body of Mary as the temple of God. Vierges Ouvrantes, popular carved images of private devotion in the later Middle Ages, combine the body of the Virgin and the body of Christ in an ingenious manner. When closed, the Madonna sits holding the Christ child upon her arm; when opened, the interior reveals either a crucifixion or Christ, sitting, holding the cross in front of his knees (Fig. 24). The interiors of the doors are often gilt and decorated with scenes of the life of Christ. Closed, they create a vaultlike womb that contains an image of Christ. Gothic cathedrals and Vierges Ouvrantes are expressions in their respective media of the same concept.[72] The pointed ribbed vault system suggests the rib cage of a gigantic mother bending over her son. The interior of the Gothic cathedral is an architectural super-Vierge Ouvrante carrying the crucified in her womb. Cathedrals increased in size until they bulged like a woman high with child. The doors, now symbols of her virginal organ, lead into the interior, which resembles a dissected female body.

The interior organization ought to be considered, then, not so much a ribbed vault in a structural sense as a rib cage in a symbolic sense. The nave vaulting overhead seems to breathe and move; the succession of vaults gives the impression of a flexible rather than a rigid system, suggesting generally the structural principles of a human ribcage (Fig. 25). This symbolism was understood as such by medieval allegorists, mystics, builders, ecclesiastics, and artists. In one of Jan Van Eyck's early paintings, *Madonna in a Church* (Kaiser Friedrich Museum, Berlin),[73] the Madonna with child is represented disproportionately large in relation to the Gothic interior, which she seems to dwarf and overpower. According to Erwin Panofsky's perceptive interpretation, "his picture represents not so much 'a Virgin Mary in a church' as 'the Virgin Mary as The Church'; not so much a human being, scaled to a real structure, as an embodiment in human form of the same spiritual force or entity that is expressed, in architectural terms, in the basilica enshrining

23 Gothic Porch and Window. Viollet-Le-Duc, *Dictionnaire Raisonné*

24 Vierge Ouvrante, French, Late XIII or Early XIV Century. Gift of J. P. Morgan, 1917, Courtesy The Metropolitan Museum of Art, New York

24

her."[74] With the inception of the Gothic style the Virgin has become the church, and the church has become the Virgin.

Seen from the west, immediately after entering the narthex of the cathedral, the crowns of French quadripartite and sexpartite vaults convey, in perspective, a continuous band of vertebrae stretching the entire length of the nave. This impressive view is reinforced by the longitudinal French web in which the individual vaults, although still undulating, are given direction by the ridge joint of the web. This longitudinal joint, evident in many cathedrals (Chartres, Sens, Nôtre Dame of Paris, Amiens, Bourges), connects the keystones and bosses of each ribbed vault and represents an incipient ridge rib, or spinal cord.

French architecture anticipated the structural function of the vault as a rib cage, but the English builders carried it to its most forceful expression. The final clarification was the introduction of the horizontal rib ridge which Francis Bond had already called the "spine" of the cathedral, but without seeing its further implications.[75] The first purely "decorative," that is, nonfunctional, ridge rib is at Lincoln Cathedral. Its interior is compelling in its suggestiveness. Nowhere has the idea of a rib cage and spinal cord been better expressed. In many English cathedrals the ridge rib ties keystone to keystone, boss to boss, or pendant to pendant. The symbolic intent of the vaulting is unmistakable, for the trumpet-shaped ribs do not seem to support the crown of the vaulting, but rather radiate down from the ridge rib, or spinal cord, as at Lincoln, Exeter, Winchester, and other cathedrals.

In English vaulting, intermediate ribs, or tiercerons, were added between the transverse and diagonal ribs. Soon after, a further element was introduced, in the form of liernes, short connecting ribs between tiercerons. Clarence Ward accounts for them in this manner: "tiercerons are not essential members of the vaulting system, and perhaps they were better omitted altogether, but that their usage can be vindicated from an aesthetic standpoint is proved by such vaults as those at Exeter. . . . [Liernes] are the result of a striving for still more complex vaulting forms and still more decorative patterns in vault construction."[76] It is highly questionable whether aesthetic values and decoration took precedent over symbolism, particularly in medieval sacred architecture. Tiercerons and liernes are not the result of a more decorative but a more symbolic striving. If the ridge

25 Anatomical Drawing of Thorax and
Shoulder Girdle

26 Winchester Nave. Banister Fletcher,
A History of Architecture

25

rib represents the spinal cord, then the transverse and diagonal ribs, as well as the
tiercerons, represent a far more naturalistic representation of a rib cage containing
the cross. The small liernes connecting tiercerons may represent intercostal
muscles running obliquely between the ribs, exactly as liernes run between
tiercerons.[77] (Fig. 26)

Beginning with Old St. Peter's, and going through the Romanesque and the
Gothic styles, it would seem as if the whole development of sacred Christian
architecture is the clarification of one basic theme—the architectural symbolization
of the incarnate Logos. The medieval cathedral exterior is an allegory of St. John's
vision of the new Jerusalem descending upon Zion, and its interior is an allegory of
the body of the Lord. The early Christian style did not have the means of expressing this allegory to its fullest extent, but the cruciform ground plan was
interpreted as a symbol of the crucified as early as the fourth century. The mature
Romanesque style is, perhaps, the most consistent expression of St. John's vision,
for it is masculine aesthetically (heavy walls and piers) and structurally (round-
headed arch), as well as symbolically (cruciform ground plan). The Gothic style,
while not abandoning the vision of St. John entirely, particularly on the exterior
facade, represents, however, a feminized interpretation of the interior aesthetically
(lightness) and structurally (pointed arch), as well as symbolically (the Virgin).
The cruciform ground plan was adhered to, but feminized elements were superimposed upon the traditional ground plan with its traditional symbolism. The

26

ALLEGORIES OF THE GOTHIC CATHEDRAL

Gothic cathedral is a compromise between ancient scriptural traditions and the victory of the cult of the Virgin Mary.

The medieval mind, overwhelmed by its own achievement, looked at the Gothic cathedral in bewilderment, as it were, and interpreted it in a lyrical fashion as a love song dedicated to the Virgin. The allegorists forgot the labor and science which constructed it and saw only symbols, beauty, and refinement. Thus they disregarded the deep conflicts not only of their own times but of their religious attitude as well.

2/THEORY OF SYMBOLISM

"It is a mistake to suppose . . . that the arts can be forever isolated from the all-encompassing march of science; from the insistence of the scientific spirit on examining every accessible realm of experience and the universe."—THOMAS MUNRO, *Towards Science in Aesthetics*

Symbol or Visual Presence?

"THE PAINTER'S PRODUCTS STAND before us as though they were alive, but if you question them, they maintain a most majestic silence" [Phaedrus, 295d.]. This statement, which Plato put into the mouth of Socrates, draws attention to one of the most vexing problems in aesthetics and symbolism—namely, to what degree do paintings communicate?

Imagine that Delacroix's *Death of Sardanapalus* was stolen from the Louvre and sold many years later to a small foreign art dealer who did not know its title and, therefore, its tragic implications. In order to facilitate its sale, he decided, after considerable reflection, to retitle it "Harem Scene." Ever after the retitling, it would seem to all those who did not know its original title to be a Dionysian orgy in which nude and partially nude women are served one by one to a sadistic oriental ruler who reclines languidly upon his elevated bed, watching his guards manhandle them to stimulate his jaded senses. A changed title will, in most cases, set up a different, if not contradictory, chain of associations of ideas. Untrained spectators will, as a rule, approach a visual presence first by the name of the artist, and second by the title; only after that may they submit themselves to aesthetic contemplation. Untitled and unidentified works rarely achieve great popularity. A sculpture of an unidentified saint, holding an unidentified symbol, stands bereft of historical, symbolic, dogmatic, and other associations and thus forces worshipers to aesthetic rather than religious contemplation. To avoid this, the Second Council of Nice (787 A.D.) declared, "But this only we should be careful of, that every image has a label, telling of what saint it is, that thus the intention of him who venerates it may be the more easily fulfilled."[1] A visual presence does not communicate with the beholder; it is the beholder who communicates with the visual presence.

Titles reinforce the illusion that paintings are symbolic. If not purely descriptive, they are either unrelated or have some occult relationship with the visual presence and are, therefore, symbolic themselves. Certain artists like to invent titles that are so remote that the title and the visual presence create tensions which the beholder has to resolve or break through. Titles, in the words of Odilon Redon, "are a kind of metaphor"[2] and can lead the mind into extraneous chains of associations of verbal symbolism.

A well-educated blind person could discourse at length about a work of art whose subject matter has been explained to him without any knowledge of its form, materials, colors, size, and so forth. Formal descriptions and analyses are measurable, verifiable, and unique with every art work. From these it will be obvious that a specific visual presence is being discussed, while from a literary, symbolic, or religious interpretation the specific work of art under discussion may not necessarily be identifiable. Even the most dramatic painting or sculpture does not scream its meaning at us, but waits silently for someone to read one into it.

We do not doubt, of course, that symbolism is a vast and profound subject; indeed, as Mircea Eliade has stated, "the history of a symbolism is a fascinating study, and one that is also fully justified, since it is the best introduction to what is called the philosophy of culture."[3] But symbolism is neither aesthetics nor art history, and symbolists, more often than not, do not care for the formal aspects of the works of art they analyze. Even the most detailed catalog of symbolic elements and interpretations tells us nothing whatsoever of aesthetic quality.

A symbolic interpretation of a work of art can be compared to the waves generated by a stone thrown into water. Following the widening circles on the surface, one soon loses sight of the stone, which meanwhile is sinking beyond recovery. Symbolic interpretations are surface interpretations, while formal ones are interpretations in depth. In short, symbolic interpretations are aftereffects of a work of art. To postulate, in addition to the aesthetic monism of form-meaning, an aesthetic dualism of form-meaning *plus* symbolism is to obscure the primarily formal nature of the visual arts.

Every visual presence is locked, physically and expressively, within its own medium. If a visual presence actually "represented" something else, it would be "instead of" that something and it would be difficult if not impossible to view it monistically. But every visual presence is a new object in the world, a new reality, subject to aesthetic laws other than the so-called reality outside of creative art. It is erroneous, therefore, to state, as Gerardus Van Der Leeuw did recently in his book *Sacred and Profane Beauty*, that "with every representation an attempt is made to approach what is represented, to hold it fast."[4] Later, however, he realized that "the bond between the representation and what is represented is not realistic, but magical."[5] Dualistic interpretations cannot free themselves of the shadows of the past, when it was believed that images were vehicles of the spirit or had oracular powers, that they could fly, were dressed, fed, beaten, or anointed; in short, that they were possessed of numinous powers. An example of a dualistic approach to a visual presence would be as follows: A visitor to Picasso's studio sees him suddenly destroy the forms of a work in progress and is shocked; he would be empathizing with the live model rather than with the visual presence.

Aesthetic monists let the form of the visual presence affect them directly without transcending ideas and associations, while aesthetic dualists emphasize ideas and associations at the expense of the form. The aims of aesthetic monism are satisfied with as complete a description of the visual presence as the critic can provide and with a visual experience of its forms. Aesthetic dualists search beyond for clues, and thus their analyses become detached from the visual presence. They are not satisfied with the existential fact of the visual presence but try to discover a teleology that is not really there. Aesthetic dualism seduces the less visually inclined critic into extensive historical, literary, psychological, symbolic, and other areas. And the farther removed the discussion is from the object, the more difficult is the road back to the visual presence.

SYMBOL OR VISUAL PRESENCE?

Clement of Alexandria, the great Christian philosopher of the second century, recognized the aesthetic quality of images while denying their symbolic values. "The Parian stone is beautiful, but it is not yet Poseidon. The ivory is beautiful, but it is not yet the Olympian Zeus. . . . Let art receive its meed of praise, but let it not deceive man by passing itself off as truth."[6] A Romanesque allegory of the Last Judgment, with devils snatching souls, threatening grotesques, and saved ones playing medieval instruments, teaches us nothing of the life to come, but much about the charged forms, gyrating movements, and ecstatic expressions created by these anonymous artists. By the same token, the panels of the Sistine Chapel teach us nothing about the origin of man, the earth, or the cosmos, but much about Michelangelo's sculptural nudes. The truths of art are the truths of form. According to Sir Herbert Read, "The whole function of art is cathartic, not didactic."[7]

It is the nature of the creative act that feelings arise of which the artist was unaware before he began the work. The aesthetic revelation of something new, therefore, is not to be considered a new symbol for something old, or an old symbol for something new, but simply an original visual presence. It is also axiomatic that a symbol must be known in order to be recognized. Furthermore, a new reality cannot be symbolic in the accepted sense of the word, because a symbol always refers to something antecedently existing, whether idea, form, or object. From this one may then draw the conclusion that visual presences do not symbolize but simply confront the beholder. The forms are not symbolic, but they may become so as an aftereffect, through a complicated psychological process which has not yet been sufficiently investigated. Interestingly enough, it takes as much effort with representational works to see form as with abstract works to see symbols. In aesthetic monism, all allusions are illusions.

The problem can be summarized as follows: That which is observed for its own properties cannot serve as a symbol, and vice versa. The moment one views objectively a visual presence (or any symbol, for that matter), it can no longer function as a symbol, for one sees only its immediate, formal presence. The less visual the beholder, or the greater his faith, in the case of religious symbols, the longer the duration of the "moment" before he discovers the formal nature of the visual presence, symbol, or object. For some it could last forever, and they would never achieve an aesthetic revelation.

SYMBOL OR VISUAL PRESENCE?

A stone carving which is believed to be the seat of a god would not be seen as a formal configuration of granite of given dimensions and specific stylistic characteristics, but when belief in its symbolic value ceases it is reinstated as a sculpture of stone. This may be analogous to contemplating a figure-ground relationship. In the Rubin Vase, for instance, when one sees the figure (vase) one does not see the ground, and when one sees the ground (two profiles) it is impossible to see the figure. To us, a blue faience ankh cross is a decorative object, since we attach no belief to it, as did the ancient Egyptians, to whom it symbolized life. It remains for us a curious antique object, although of aesthetic significance. Another example is the cross. It may consist of two planks of wood of given lengths and widths, hardness and texture. It becomes a symbol of the Passion only if it is known as such or is believed in. As long as one is ignorant of its meaning, or as long as one sees it as two mounted planks, it cannot function as a sacred symbol. And when one sees it as a symbol, one does not see it objectively in its material properties. Either aspect blocks the other. (Fig. 27)

We have sufficient distance from the arts of past and alien civilizations to see them as visual presences rather than as symbols. If we habitually see more recent art forms still in terms of symbols, we will have to re-educate our eyes toward a more direct visual experience. In the words of Seurat: "They see poetry in what I have done. No, I apply my method, and that is all there is to it."[8]

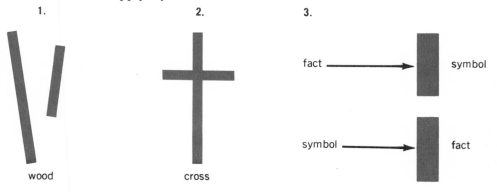

27   Diagram of Cross as Symbol or Fact

The Symbolism of Nonobjective Art

"TRUTH IN ART is the unity of a thing with itself: the outward rendered expressive of the inward; the soul made incarnate; the body instinct with spirit."[1] This dictum by Oscar Wilde applies eminently to nonobjective art, which was able to achieve this unity by making the leap from the spirit to the canvas without the intervening step of subject matter. Nonobjective art starts where representational art leaves off. It has the advantage that it does not wrestle with representational elements in addition to spiritual ones, but with spiritual ones alone. Nonobjective art, in the hands of its masters, has torn the veil from visible nature and presented its animating forces in the process of creation out of chaos or rest.

Nonobjective art was the external manifestation of a spiritual revolution that did not materialize, except in art. Conceptionally it was precipiated by Theosophy, a self-styled universal religion founded in New York in 1875 which aimed at a spiritual revitalization of the West. Its antirationalism had a certain appeal for those who were dissatisfied with the intense materialism and scientism of the late nineteenth century. Theosophy offered instead a mystic, oriental interpretation of life and evolution. According to Sophia Wadia, a Hindu Theosophical leader, "It was Theosophy which alone linked East and West, and made the work of spreading spiritual knowledge all over the world imperative and possible."[2] During the forty years of its greatest influence (1875–1915) it made a deep impression on the thinking of many leading scientists (Flammarion), philosophers (Rudolph Steiner), scholars (Max Müller), writers (Maeterlinck), musicians (Scriabin), and artists (Kandinsky and Mondrian).

It is on this Theosophic foundation that Kandinsky and Mondrian formed their aesthetic theories. As Kandinsky wrote in *On the Spiritual in Art*: "Literature, music and art are the first sensitive spheres in which this spiritual revolution makes itself felt, in the form of reality. These spheres reflect immediately the dark picture of the present; they feel the immensity of what, at first, was only a minute point of light, noticed by few and ignored by the vast majority."[3]

Theosophy taught the ancient Hindu doctrines of the interpenetration of the spiritual and physical realms: that the material appearance of nature is but an illusion (*maya*) and that there are several sheaths or bodies of progressively more spiritual matter within every individual. It also popularized the concept that the individual soul (*atman*) is identical with the oversoul (*Brahman*). The soul is but a divine traveler on an infinite round of cumulative experiences, from the lowest, the inorganic kingdom, to the highest, past man and superman, to return, finally, to *Brahman*. This spiritual Darwinism seemed very attractive to many who saw more in nature than just physical phenomena, and it proved extremely inspiring to certain painters to whom the doctrine of the spiritual nature of all things opened up vast possibilities of experimentation with organic and inorganic forms, for in the Hindu pantheism everything contains a soul, not only man, but the lowest animal, plant, and crystal as well.

The esoteric and pseudoscientific aspects of Theosophy together with the many scandals connected with its founder, the Russian Helena Petrovna Blavatsky,[4] created much animosity, and, except in insignificant splinter groups, it did not survive the First World War. However, Kandinsky (who respectfully mentions Helena Petrovna Blavatsky in his book), faithful to Theosophic principles, believed that "each one of these artists, who can see beyond the limits of his present stage, in this segment of spiritual evolution is a prophet to those surrounding him and helps to move forward the ever obstinate carload of humanity."[5] The acknowledged father of Abstract Expressionism arrived at his style and theory of art through mystic intuitions. He made this clear in his classic treatise *On the Spiritual in Art.*

> *The form, even if entirely abstract and resembling a geometric figure, has its inner harmony and is a spiritual being with characteristics identical to it . . . (p. 46).*

> *It is clear, therefore, that this choice of object (one of the elements in the harmony of form) must be decided only by the corresponding vibration in the human soul . . . (p. 51).*

> *His eye should be directed to his inner life and his ear should hearken to the words of inner necessity. Then, he will resort with equal ease to every means and achieve his end. This is the only way to express the mystic need . . . (p. 58).*

> *That is to be considered beautiful which results from an inner spiritual need, as only that which is spiritual can be beautiful . . . (p. 95).*

Similarly, Mondrian lived under the spell of Theosophy. He joined the Theosophical Society of Amsterdam in 1909, but had evinced interest in its doctrines years before that.[6] His thought was profoundly influenced by the books of a Dutch Theosophist M. H. J. Shoenmakers. "It is evident in many places that Mondrian borrowed from him a part of the terminology that appears in the essays published later in *De Stijl*. Unquestionably he took from him the main term *nieuwe beelding*, which we may translate literally as 'new form-construction'—more commonly called neo-plasticism."[7] Mondrian's vision, although the purest of its genre, can be related to Cubism. He recognized the latent possibilities in Cubism and brought to it a vision which matched the potential of its form.

As early as 1914, Mondrian wrote in his notebooks thoughts which antedate those published in *De Stijl* and which show the direction of his aesthetic and mystical thinking.

> *Two roads lead to the spiritual: the road of doctrinal teaching, of direct*

exercise (meditation, etc.) and the slow but certain road of evolution. One sees in art the slow growth of spirituality, of which the artists themselves are unconscious.

To approach the spiritual in art, one will use as little of reality as possible, for reality is opposed to the spiritual. Thus the use of elementary forms is quite logical. Since these forms are abstract, we find ourselves confronted by an art that is abstract.

Art, being superhuman, cultivates the superhuman element in man and hence has become a means for humanity's evolution of equal importance with religion.

The artist by intuition sees things much more spiritually than do ordinary men. That is why the reality he sees is more beautiful, and for the same reason art is a boon to ordinary men.[8]

Mondrian wanted above all to catch the "pulsating rhythm of life." He wrote in *New Art—New Life*: "The exact expression of the rhythm of equivalent oppositions [horizontal and vertical] is able to enhance our sense of *the value of the vital rhythm* in a most thorough way, through its new representation, to make us somewhat aware of the actual tenor of life."[9] The equivalence of these two straight lines, horizontal and vertical, indicated to him the two aspects of life, the equal value of matter and spirit, masculine and feminine, collective and individual, in short, "the profound rhythm of all that exists."[10]

What some see today in terms of pure aesthetic was to Mondrian (and Kandinsky as well) an expression of pure spirit. Mondrian's grid system was born of his monistic theory of the cosmos, for he believed that the manifested universe is an illusion and that everything is spirit. His neutral background is the undifferentiated continuum, the void, or Nirvana. Within this cosmic void the absolute plays its cosmic game of creating and destroying, manifesting and disappearing, becoming and resting. He hoped to break through the visible into the eternal. He rejected nature not only because it was to him an illusion but because it is the ever-changing manifestation of a constant principle he called spirit. This we find confirmed in Mondrian's early notebooks. "The positive and

the negative break up oneness, they are the cause of all unhappiness. . . .
The union of the positive and the negative is happiness. The more the positive
and the negative are united in a being, the happier he will be. . . . Art being
life, it depends on the state of evolution and on the nature of society. Since modern
science has confirmed the Theosophical doctrine according to which matter
and force (mind) are *one*, there is no reason to separate them. If it is true that
matter and mind (force) constitute life, we must take both into account and
not just one of these two. . . ."[11]

    This theory of the oneness of life (monism) Mondrian culled from those classic
Hindu scriptures popularized in the West by Theosophy—the Upanishads
and the Bhagavad Gita.

> *This whole world the illusion-maker* (mayin) *projects out of this [Brahma].*
>
> *And in it by illusion* (maya) *the other [individual soul] is confined.*
>
> *Now, one should know that Nature (Prakriti) is illusion* (maya),
>
> *And that the Mighty Lord* (mahesvara) *is the illusion-maker* (mayin). . . .[12]
>
> *The Lord of all things living; not the less—*
> *By Maya, by magic which I stamp*
> *On floating Nature-forms, the primal vast—*
> *I come, and go, and come. . . .[13]*

    We know that Kandinsky and Mondrian derived their theoretical background
from Theosophy; mandalas may have given them certain formal elements.
Since Mondrian indicated in his early notebooks that he believed in meditation
practices, it is more than likely that he was familiar with these mystic
diagrams of oriental religions. A mandala is a magic circle or square (or a square
within a circle) drawn on paper or on the ground, or made of butter, rice,
and other materials. It is an abstract pattern upon which the devotee, monk, or
yogin meditates, for the center of the mandala is believed to be the seat of a
deity. It is believed that during meditation these mandalas become charged with

immense power and the deity appears before the mental eye of the devotee. He identifies with it and often imagines that he himself is the god to whose perfection he aspires.[14] Mandalas are also used in magic by lamas to acquire superhuman powers, or *siddhis*.[15] Such mandalas have been used in the East from time immemorial and are evidence of the oriental antecedence of the theory that abstract patterns are charged with energy or spiritual forces. (Fig. 28) Certain remarks by Kandinsky confirm his belief in the latent spiritual powers of geometric designs: "we recognize the spirit of our time in the realm of construction, not as clear 'geometric' construction, which is immediately noticeable, rich in possibilities and expressive, but as an inscrutable one, which inadvertently lifts itself beyond painting; and which, therefore, is meant less for the eye than for the soul."[16] And Mondrian: "When one does not represent things, a place remains for the divine. . . ."[17] Mondrian, in particular, achieved with his paintings what a yogin achieves in deep meditation—the reconciliation of all opposites and the mergence into Nirvana.

The severe grid system of Mondrian's style profoundly affected international architecture, interior decoration, commercial art, typography, and other fields of creative endeavor. Kandinsky, on the other hand, freed the artist's subconscious and substantially altered the history of painting toward a direct translation of the artist's intuition of the inner forces of nature. We are today surrounded by symbols of the equivalence of spirit and matter. But this is exactly what was desired by these artists for whom art was an implement in the evolution of man toward a greater awareness of the world of the spirit. It was with this larger purpose in mind that Kandinsky wrote: "Anyone who absorbs the innermost hidden treasures of art, is an enviable partner in building the spiritual pyramid, which is meant to reach into heaven."[18] Mondrian echoed this same feeling 21 years later: "after all there is only *one way of evolution, absolutely identical as to life and to art*."[19]

The founders of the nonobjective styles of art either identified with mystical movements or thought in terms of extreme subjective idealism, aesthetically as well as philosophically. Just to think of "pure form," "pure space," or "conceptual spaces" implies speculations of a mathematical and philosophical order. Of course, not all nonobjective painters are mystics, but all strive toward

28 Hindu Meditation Mandala. Heinrich
Zimmer, *Myths and Symbols in
Indian Art and Civilization* (New
York, 1946), Plate 36

28

a purer vision and toward direct self-expression. Kasimir Malevich, for instance, was no mystic, but he too aimed at a purer vision, at a complete liberation from "things" and a feeling for the "essence." Suprematism, according to Malevich, is an "unmasked" art from which to contemplate life through the prism of pure aesthetic feelings. In other words, suprematism is a "concretion of feeling."[20] Zen Buddhism has the same significance for the younger American Abstract Expressionists that Theosophy had for the founders. And those who have no leaning toward mysticism embrace existentialism, which, like subjective idealism, leads to solipsism, the point at which oriental mysticism and extreme individualism touch. Robert Motherwell, summing up the position of the younger American nonobjective painters, said: "For make no mistake, abstract art is a form of mysticism . . . [it] is an effort to close the void that modern men feel. . . . I think that one's art is just one's effort to wed oneself to the universe, to unify oneself through union. . . ."[21] Representational painters who identify with nature achieve, in some instances, a state of *participation mystique*; nonobjective artists aim toward *participation créatif*, for they identify with the creative forces of nature.

Since the middle of the nineteenth century, artists have been experimenting with a more and more synthetic view of the world. Several schools arose that tried to express nature in terms of light and pure color (Impressionism and Expressionism), in terms of pure space (Cubism), in terms of pure mathematical relationships (Neo-Plasticism), in psychological terms (Surrealism), and, finally, in extreme subjectivity (Abstract Expressionism). The history of the destruction of the outer world of appearance signifies a gradual spiritualization of art, for it leads to ever more symbolic statements. The fact that these symbols are often of an intensely personal nature does not necessarily weaken this contention, for the spiritual experience of twentieth-century man has also, to a large degree, become a private one. "Man's ultimate concern must be expressed symbolically, because symbolic language alone is able to express the ultimate."[22] This applies, as well, to pictorial language, for when art falls short of ultimate concern, that is, the painter's interpretation of the cosmos, it belongs in the category of "signs," or forms which are easily recognized but which do not evoke a deeper, spiritual response in the viewer. The evocative

29 Jackson Pollock, #5, 1950. Gift of
Mr. and Mrs. Walter Bareiss,
Courtesy The Museum of Modern
Art, New York

powers of a symbol transcend language, for its connotations may be infinite.
In short, a symbol is "something that stands for, represents, or denotes something
else . . . *esp.* a material object representing, or taken to represent, something
immaterial or abstract, as a being, idea, quality or condition."[23]

When one contemplates a nonobjective painting by Jackson Pollock, for
example, one experiences the forces themselves that gave rise to it, for the
creative idea which engendered the canvas is the painting itself; in other words,
the aesthetic components are also its spiritual elements (Fig. 29). In the Abstract
Expressionist Style, for the first time in the history of art, there is no dichotomy
between matter and spirit, or form and meaning, for they have fused.
This is a tremendous step into a new dimension of art and experience necessitating
a reevaluation of symbolism in nonobjective art.

Since a symbol, by definition, stands for something other than itself (the
lotus symbolizes purity; yang-yin, heaven and earth; the circle, eternity; light,
God, and so forth), paintings which constitute a direct experience may not
rightly be considered symbolic. Intuitive insights do not depend upon intermediate
steps such as verbal or visual symbols; they are direct apprehensions of reality.
The difference between symbolization and direct experience may be compared
to a painting of an apple and the eating of it. Verbal description of an apple
is the farthest removed from reality; a painting of it is somewhat related to
reality, but only in eating can an apple actually be experienced. When the act
of painting is the aesthetic, or spiritual, experience (action painting), it cannot
be interpreted symbolically. The viewer does not stand in front of such a canvas
searching for symbols, he has a direct impact of the reality itself. Nonobjective
paintings are shortcuts to experience, eliminating two important steps which
are essential in language and representational art. The classic procedure was:
1) object or idea, 2) the symbol, i.e., the painting, 3) the viewer. Now there
are only 1) the painting and 2) the viewer. Consistently nonobjective paintings
depend upon neither object nor symbol. What is left is a direct experience of a
reality confronting the viewer.

Nonobjective art has broken through the process of symbolization itself. The cardinal point of difference between nonobjective and representational art is that in the former the formal referents are not symbols in the traditional sense, evoking something outside themselves, but that they are simply without denotative content altogether. The mature paintings of Kandinsky, Mondrian, or Pollock remind one of nothing ever seen in this world. And new forms create new emotions with which we have to become acquainted. Nonobjective art has made an important contribution to the history of the development of the mind, opening up new dimensions of perception and being. Infinity becomes larger each time a new style adds a new extension. It has been the historical purpose of art to enlarge our dimensions of seeing, and therefore of knowing, and to transfigure them with the magic of artistic expression.

Although nonobjective art cannot properly be called symbolic, the term is almost unavoidable, for even the mathematical purity of Mondrian's paintings or the swirling, energetic dimensions of Pollock's have physical characteristics and emotional suggestiveness. They exist in a twilight zone between form and spirit. The only way we can discuss them without falling into the symbolic or semantic trap would be with a new term which cuts across both form and spirit—metasymbolic. The term metasymbolism emphasizes the fact that the conformations of nonobjective art are symbolic only of themselves.

The difference between "symbolic" and "metasymbolic" may be formulated as follows: all works of art which evoke something other than themselves are symbolic (representational or partly representational art works which portray nudes, trees, guitars, waves, and so forth, since the objects themselves are obviously not *upon* the canvas or *in* the stone), but all those works of art which do not symbolize anything outside of themselves should be considered metasymbolic.

The epistemological problem is the critic's, not the artist's. The artist's epistemology is in the act of creating, which is a valid, although nonverbal, form of knowledge. The moment art abandoned nature, the task of the critic became problematic, for most abstract paintings defy description. As Susanne K. Langer put it. "Non-discursive symbols cannot be defined in terms of others, as discursive symbols can."[24] The greatest difficulty arises with metasymbolic

30 Piet Mondrian, Composition #2,
    1922, Paris. Courtesy The Solomon
    R. Guggenheim Museum, New York

30

paintings which transcend even visual, nondiscursive symbolism as defined above. Metasymbolism also requires a new language, a metaesthetics which emphasizes the creative process revealed upon the canvas, eschewing any reference whatsoever to verbal or visual images. The originators of nonobjective art believed that the forms and colors which they employed were a priori charged with spiritual content that would evoke a corresponding spiritual response in the "soul" of the observer. The infinite calm of a Mondrian is as explicit and clear a statement as is humanly possible (Fig. 30). The same applies to the other extreme as represented by Kandinsky, Pollock, and others, where a visual condensation of lines, forms, and colors takes place before the eyes of the observer. Mondrian's world, in which all tensions have come to rest and all opposites have been equalized, and Pollock's world, which is still in the process of evolving, are deeply moving and compelling spiritual-aesthetic insights.

It is regrettable that some critics have attacked nonobjective art as expressions of "terror," "chaos," "perverted visual trends," "spectacles of a continuous nervous breakdown," "nihilistic automatism," "mechanical arrangements," and so on. This amounts, of course, to nothing more than name-calling, and it evades the profound problems raised by these forms. Critics, trained in the classic tradition of scholarship and seeing, naturally feel baffled and robbed of time-honored standards. But when they "interpret" in direct opposition to the declared intentions of the artist they face a burden of proof they cannot objectively deliver.[25] On the other hand, the pomander-scented prose of certain of the younger writers who vigorously defend it is equally wide of the mark. No verbal gymnastics will make its mysteries more comprehensible precisely because one symbolism cannot be substituted for another. The factors involved in criticism of nonobjective art are six: historic, technical, aesthetic, philosophic, metasymbolic, and semantic. Of these, the first four admit of intelligible discussion, while the last two defy it. One is reminded of the terse statement by the philosopher Ludwig Wittgenstein: "whereof one cannot speak thereof one must be silent."[26]

Symbolism and Allegory

WILLIAM DURANDUS, the thirteenth-century Bishop of Mende and one of the leading allegorists of his time, gives a curious interpretation of a certain custom practiced in some local churches.

> In some churches two eggs of ostriches and other things which cause
>   admiration, and which are rarely seen, are accustomed to be suspended:
>   that by their means the people may be drawn to church, and have
>   their minds the more affected. Again, some say that the ostrich,
>   as being a forgetful bird, "leaveth her eggs in the dust": and at length,
>   when she beholdeth a certain star, returneth unto them, and cheereth
>   them by her presence. Therefore the eggs of ostriches are hung in
>   churches to signify that man, being left of God on account of
>   his sins, if at length he be illuminated by the Divine Light, remembereth
>   his faults and returneth to Him, Who by looking on him with His
>   Mercy cherisheth him. As it is written in Luke that after Peter had
>   denied Christ, the "Lord turned and looked upon Peter." Therefore

*be the aforesaid eggs suspended in churches, this signifying, that man
easily forgetteth God, unless being illuminated by a star, that is,
by the Influence of the Holy Spirit, he is reminded to return
to Him by good works.*[1]

It is obvious from the above that Durandus does not know why ostrich eggs
were suspended in some churches; not knowing, he falls back on and embellishes
those remarks about ostriches and their eggs as he has read about them in
Mediaeval Bestiaries derived from Physiologus.[2] What we stress here is that
from the Durandus allegory alone we could not reconstruct the original
historical, ritualistic, or other reasons why ostrich eggs were exhibited in
some churches. (Among several possibilities are that the eggs may have
served as a symbol of the Immaculate Conception of Christ, since the Bestiaries
tell that the ostrich abandons its eggs to be hatched by the sun; or as symbols
of the Resurrection, of Divine Love, or of fertility. They could even refer to
Leda, who laid two eggs after Zeus embraced her in the form of a swan; or
they might have been simply *curiosa* brought back by the Crusaders.[3])

Trying to reconstruct from an allegory the primary concept, symbol, or ritual
to which it refers is like opening an Easter egg—one never knows the surprise
it contains. The surprise is, of course, unrelated to the container. The reason
for this is that an allegory is a symbol for a symbol. Symbols, at one time,
could hint at vast potentials dimly felt. They could enlarge man's intuitions
by their suggestiveness, but allegories lose that power in their circuitous routes
of inverted thinking. The great allegories with which the medieval mind
was preoccupied, from the New Jerusalem to the unicorn, have died, while
many primary symbols, such as the cross and aureola, still linger on, by sheer
force of tradition, by belief, or as forms in the figurative arts. If symbols
serve as stepping stones to abstract concepts, allegories are rather like jigsaw
puzzles with missing pieces.[4]

Symbols fall into several classes. A so-called iconic symbol (identity
between form and idea) requires no leap of imagination or intuition from the
symbol to the concept because one sees, feels, or experiences that the flame
is heat, blood is life, the wheel is motion, the skull is death, the hammer is power,
the phallus is procreation, and so forth. A noniconic symbol (no identity

between form and idea) requires one leap, from the symbol to the concept, such as the wheel cross for a member of the Trinity, the anchor for salvation, the fish for Christ, seven golden rays for seven gifts of the Holy Spirit, and the enclosed garden for the Virgin Mary, among others. Since symbol and concept are not related in a noniconic symbol, the leap of the mind accomplishes an occult relationship between the two. An allegory, on the other hand, requires two or more leaps, but, interestingly enough, the leaps must be made in reverse from the allegory through the secondary to the primary symbol or concept. For example, in Hans Memling's painting *Virgin and Child* (Metropolitan Museum of Art, J. H. Bache Collection, 1949), the Virgin daintily holds an apple while the Christ child sitting in front of her reaches toward it (Fig. 31). This seemingly harmless and playful detail allegorizes Mary as the second Eve and Christ as the second Adam. In other words, the apple in her hand signifies that while Adam and Eve brought sin into the world, Mary and Christ removed it. Viewing this allegorical painting requires quite a leap backwards via the noniconic symbol of the apple (seduction, fertility) and beyond that to Adam and Eve, who, according to the Old Testament, committed the original sin.

If the meaning of an allegory is not known beforehand, according to the rule of Hugh of St. Victor (twelfth century), it is not possible to leap from the allegory to the primary concept. He put it this way:

> ... the New Testament, in which the evident truth is preached, is, in the study, placed before the Old, in which the same truth is announced in a hidden manner, shrouded in figures. It is the same truth in both places, but hidden there, open here, promised there, shown here. You have heard, in the reading from the Apocalypse (5:5) that the book was sealed and no one could be found who should loose its seals save only the Lion of the tribe of Judah. The Law was sealed, sealed were the prophecies, because the times of the redemption to come were announced in a hidden manner. ... And in order not to risk making this tedious to you by following through each item [from the Old Testament]: unless you know beforehand the nativity of Christ, his teaching, his suffering, his resurrection and ascension, and all

31   Hans Memling, The Virgin and
     Child. The Jules S. Bache Collection,
     1949, Courtesy The Metropolitan
     Museum of Art, New York

*the other things which he did in the flesh and through the flesh, you
will not be able to penetrate the mysteries of the old figures.*[5]

One may attempt to leap from an allegory backward to the primary symbol,
ritual, or concept, but one leaps into the dark, often with disastrous results.

   The *locus classicus* of medieval allegorism is the Song of Solomon.
This somewhat erotic Old Testament love poem, in which Solomon celebrates
his love for Shulamith, was allegorized by the church Fathers as a chaste
song in which Christ sings of his love for his church.[6] St. Bernard of Clairvaux,
however, applied the figures of speech which were used in reference to
Shulamith to the Virgin Mary. With great imagination and no little effort, the
Song of Solomon was changed into its opposite. In this and similar instances,
an allegory can transform black to white and vice versa. On the other hand, a
contemporary of Solomon who was familiar with his infatuation with Shulamith
could not possibly have interpreted his song in allegorical terms, referring
to entirely different events occurring one thousand years later, as Hugh of
St. Victor clearly stated. But the medieval allegorists disregarded his insight in
favor of an entirely artificial method of interpretation amounting to intellectual,
if not spiritual, sleight of hand. Thus the famous fifteenth-century theologian
Jean Petit taught: "In the Holy Scripture, the literal sense is false."[7] And in
the Prologue to the *Speculum Humanae Salvationis*, the ambiguities of the
allegorical method are spelled out: "Thus the same thing may signify at
one time the devil, at another Christ. Nor should we marvel at this mode of
Scripture in which according to the deeds or actions of a person diverse
meanings can be attributed to him. . . ."[8]

   In the figurative arts allegories detract from the nature of the object,
for as we hunt for the key we lose the visual aspects of form, style, and technique.
Art in the service of allegory becomes something else, namely, a labyrinth
of verbal meanings which are extraneous to visual form. For instance, the

fourteenth-century sculpture of the Virgin of Nôtre Dame of Paris (interior
nave in front of the choir) stands upon a base decorated with a mermaid (Fig. 32).
The mermaid is carved in a style quite different from the manneristic and
stiff Madonna supporting the Christ child on her arm. It seems incongruous
with the nature of the subject to find this fantastic creature associated with
the Madonna and Child. The classic style of the mermaid, with its rounded
forms and sinuous position, derives from and refers to something non-Christian
in content and pre-Christian in style. We know, of course, of the survival
of classical themes in medieval art.[9] Also, certain motifs were copied by
medieval sculptors from such fragments as had survived the Roman occupation
of Gaul. Most likely this mermaid under the Virgin of Nôtre Dame fulfilled
a more decorative than symbolic function. (Fantastic subject matter was often
carved on misericords, keystones, and choir stalls of churches.) Mermaids fall into
the genus of Sirens, who in classic times were believed to bewitch sailors
with their sweet voices so that they met with death in approaching their rocky
island dwellings. Some allegorists, however, could not resist reinterpreting
even this motif, and instead of being a symbol of danger, seduction, and death
she became in their hands an allegory of the two natures of Christ. In a Cornish
drama, *Passio Domini*, the second half of the fourteenth-century trilogy
Ordinalia, two doctors argue about the human and divine natures of Christ,
one of them defending the argument with the mermaid allegory: "Look at
the mermaid/ Half fish and half human,/ His being God and Man clearly,/
To that same thing credence we give."[10]

   If we did not know of this allegory, the mermaid would simply be a mythological
motif decorating the base of the Virgin of Nôtre Dame, reminiscent of the
many statues of Christ standing upon basilisks or other fantastic creatures,
signifying that evil has been overcome by good. Knowledge of the mermaid
allegory confuses the concept of Christ rather than clarifies it, since a
mermaid is a Siren with ancient associations of death and since she is a female
creature allegorizing a male God. Even the most sophisticated interpretive
techniques are meaningless when an allegory is a false (etiological) explanation

of a fact or ritual long since forgotten, when there is no documentation as to the intention of the allegory, when it conceals rather than explains, or when the key is buried with the artist or patron.

There are universal symbols, like the sun for God, water for purity, or blood for life, but there are no universal allegories.[11] There are universal iconic symbols in which there is an identity between the form and the concept. Noniconic symbols, being arbitrary, cannot be validated and are neither universal nor self-explanatory. In short, allegories are artificial constructs and tend to mislead rather than to lead. One cannot question the validity of iconic symbols, but one can rightfully question all noniconic symbols and allegories.

No sign or symbol has a power beyond that assigned to it, more or less arbitrarily, by a culture. This basic fact cannot be stated too often or too forcefully. Yet ancient, almost forgotten occult traditions and modern sentimentalities tend to endow certain traditional symbols with magical, psychological, and other powers which symbols cannot possess by themselves. Some contemporary scholars and psychologists, however, claim that traditional symbols which must be learned anew by each generation lead a secret inner life which, under certain circumstances, can be reawakened. In this sense the French scholar René Guénon wrote: "It should be noted that symbols always retain their proper value, even when traced without conscious intention, as occurs when certain symbols, no longer understood, are preserved merely by way of ornamentation."[12] That this theory is not borne out by fact can be demonstrated by confronting a large group of people with a variety of prehistoric symbols of the Indus Valley, South American, and Tibetan religions. Since the majority will be ignorant of them (even specialists do not as yet understand the meaning of most Indus Valley, pre-Buddhist Tibetan, and Mayan symbols), they cannot be understood in "their proper value," and interest will shift to aesthetic contemplation of their form rather than recognition of their alleged psychic content. There is nothing in symbols themselves which speaks to us directly, with the exception of self-explanatory iconic symbols in which the concept is inherent in the form.

The criticism of Paul Tillich's position by Dr. John W. Dixon, Jr., is justified: "Paul Tillich, for example, is fond of asserting that the symbol participates in the reality it symbolizes, yet never makes clear what this participation entails."[13] Tillich's remark is particularly open to question when one recalls symbols of prehistoric and forgotten religions or of Gnosticism and Mithraism which have faded from the consciousness of society. That there is an Egyptian term Ka and its bird symbol is no guarantee that the shadow soul which they symbolized actually existed. In what sense, then, did the Ka participate in the "reality" it symbolized? Similarly, astrological symbols like Pisces, Taurus, Virgo, Aquarius, and so forth are only Gestalt phenomena projected into the sky by the ancient Babylonians. If they actually existed, the centrally located sun would have to move rather rapidly in a gigantic circle through the so-called twelve houses or signs of the Zodiac. This is a prescientific visual illusion, seen from the rotating earth, to which inordinate symbolic significance has been assigned as to the relationships between the positions of the planets and man's talents, disposition, and fate. One can make a symbol of anything, but only at the expense of its objective reality or by inventing a symbol like the Ka which may have no reality at all. To say that everything is significant or meaningful is not the same as saying that everything is symbolic. If the latter were true, everything would seem something other than what it is.

Any symbol may be compared to a lens with a sliding scale of opaqueness. The more the symbol is taken as a reality, the more opaque it will become, so that in the end only the symbol itself is visible; it does not permit any view through it to the concept. On the other hand, the more it is recognized as merely an aid to conceptualization, the more transparent a symbol will become, until it vanishes altogether, as the viewer is confronted by the phenomenon itself.

Symbolism is a dangerous path, which one must tread with care. The elemental needs of man are satisfied directly without symbols. However, while symbols have opened to man the path of speculative thinking and have led to his breathtaking cultural development, they have alienated him from nature. On one extreme is the world of animals without the capacity to symbolize; on the other is the world of man, "the uniquely symbol-using organism,"[14] with the built-in danger of developing a too symbolic universe. Medieval man estranged himself from reality by interpreting practically every phenomenon in symbolic or allegoric terms. One cannot excuse medieval allegorists as naive or ignorant. On the contrary, some of the most learned men made the greatest efforts in this direction and deliberately encouraged the grotesque and fantastic at the expense of the natural.

Eugene Bleuler, the famous Swiss psychiatrist, concluded that "the patterns of medieval thought afford many points of comparison with schizophrenia. During that period too, thought processes had autistically turned away from reality; the conclusions of thought processes were not the result of logical operations; rather, the conclusions were affectively predetermined judgements and logic was used to the extent only that it led to the desired end. . . ."[15] A leading contemporary American psychiatrist, Silvano Arieti, corroborates Bleuler in that he warns of the dangers of private symbols (which he calls paleosymbols) which are unverifiable and have much in common with the allegorical interpretations of medieval thinkers. "In paleosymbols, the image may be substituted by an external object, gesture or sound. But these externalizations are chosen arbitrarily by the individual. Therefore they may lead to fatal errors. . . . The paleosymbol is more definite than the image, but is also highly individual, subjective, emotionally loaded and unverifiable."[16] Both Bleuler (p. 351) and Arieti (p. 327) state that in schizophrenics the distinction between imagination and reality is certainly reduced altogether; in other words, the mentally ill reinterpret reality.

Thus the allegorical world is an artificial world, its dangers only too evident. Bleuler condemned medieval symbolism as schizophrenic; perhaps he goes a little too far, but, to paraphrase Géza Róheim, the more extreme medieval symbolists and allegorists were certainly schizophrenics *manqués*.[17]

The path of symbolism, in spite of its potential for increasing awareness, can also lead from reality into the dark world of the private fantasy universe. The development of science is a gradual retreat from the symbolic, mythopoeic, and magical interpretations of the cosmos in favor of the empirical and descriptive study of phenomena. "His [Husserl's] repeated insistence upon a return to experience is not merely a desire to achieve direct contact with objectivity rather than with its symbols; it is rather an insistent demand on a validation of experience itself, without which any further cognition can be only imperfectly rational."[18] Ernst Cassirer arrived at a similar conclusion: "Physical reality seems to recede in proportion as man's symbolic activity advances."[19] The medieval world view proves that the destruction of reality begins in symbolism and ends in allegory.

A Sixfold Schema of Symbolism

THE WORLD "SYMBOL" stems from the Greek *symballo*, to throw together, join, or unite. It derives from the ancient custom of *symbola*, which were signs of recognition between a host and his guests.[1] The host would break an earthenware object or a ring and distribute some of the pieces to his guests. He would retain some of the remaining fragments. When host and guests met again, the broken pieces would be joined together and served as a sign of recognition. A symbol, in its original context, was a secret sign of recognition, since only the pieces held by the host and particular guests would fit together to make a meaningful whole. This implies that the pieces, or the idea and its symbol, must perfectly correspond to each other. Notwithstanding primitive usage, where anything could serve as a symbol of the numinous, not all symbols are commensurate with the ideas they symbolize.

Symbols are not created by gifted individuals but are the anonymous expressions of mankind that reach back into prehistory. Creative art is personal; symbols are impersonal. They have no pathos, and their appeal is neither strictly formal nor self-expressive. The moment a symbol attracts attention

to itself, it has either been transformed into art or become magical. As Jane
Harrison puts it, "What might have been an ideal becomes an idol."[2] This
was the fate of many symbols which were believed to be imbued with "virtues."
Nor does a symbol need to be executed in a exquisite formal manner. A rude
graffito, such as the anchor cross in the Catacombs, is sufficient to evoke to
a believer that "other," the abstract concept for which it stands. A creative work
of art exists on so many levels—formal, ideational, and symbolic—that its
complexity alone lifts it beyond mere symbolism. Susanne K. Langer expresses
this succinctly: "Artistic forms are more complex than any other symbolic
forms we know."[3] Works of art that are predominantly symbolic tend to
fail as pure aesthetic forms.

Most symbols, unfortunately, do not have just one definite meaning but
are susceptible to various interpretations. They can be read in contradictory
terms. The fish symbol, for example, may be female (Venus) or male (Christ);
the pig, clean or unclean; the serpent, wise or evil; the rose could represent
passion or purity; the cross, life or death; the dove, sexuality or the Holy Ghost.
Also, ignorance of the meaning of a specific symbol may lead to erroneous
ex post facto explanations or etiological myths. A curious instance of this is
the famous IHS. Originally, this monogram derived from the first three Greek
letters of the name Iesous. Another, later interpretation, ascribed to Constantine's
vision before his battle against Maxentius, interprets the same three letters
to mean *In Hoc Signo* [*Vinces*]. In its Latinized form this monogram also yields
the popular version, *Jesus Hominum Salvator*. More recently, the same letters
were interpreted in English to mean "I Have Suffered," and also "I Have
Saved." A German version is *Jesus Heiland Seligmacher*. This is but one instance
of five different concurrent interpretations of the same symbol.

Symbols are kept alive as long as belief in their efficacy and power breathes
life into them. When faith in a symbol is lost—that is, in the concept for
which it stands—it will automatically become meaningless. We are reminded
of the symbols of Gnosticism which once promised immortality but are now
just the lifeless debris of a forgotten religion. This phenomenon was clearly
recognized by Dean Inge. "It is the tendency of all symbols to petrify or
evaporate, and either process is fatal to them. They soon repudiate their

mystical origin, and forthwith lose their religious content."[4]

The transformation of abstract (aniconic) symbols into figurative ones is characterized by an increase in the realism and sensuality with which they are depicted. This process also implies a gradual loss of the concept for which the symbol stands. This principle can be verified with the development of the cross. At first only a plain cross was depicted, then a cross with a lamb, and finally a cross with the corpus. The Seventh General Council (*in Trullo*), 692 A.D., decreed that icons which represented the lamb should thenceforth represent the crucified. "In order therefore that 'that which is perfect' may be delineated to the eyes of all, at least in colored expression, we decree that the figure in human form of the Lamb who taketh away the sin of the world, Christ our God, be henceforth exhibited in images instead of the ancient lamb, so that all may understand by means of it the depth of the humiliation of the Word of God, and that we may recall to our memory his conversation in the flesh, his passion and solitary death, and his redemption which was wrought for the whole world." (Canon LXXXII)[5]

The crucifixion appears during the fifth century A.D. and is of the so-called triumphant type. The famous wooden panel of S. Sabina, in Rome, shows an erect male figure with slightly outstretched arms, flanked by two smaller figures in similar attitudes. No crosses are present, however, and this may represent a transitional or hesitant attempt to represent this scene. The ivory panel from a casket, in the British Museum, also of the fifth century, is probably the first unmistakable crucifixion, for in it are the cross, the inscription, John, Mary, the legionnaire, and Judas hanging from a tree. Such examples are rare before the eighth century and were often greeted with astonishment. "In sixth-century France the painting of Christ on the Cross in a church still excited such scandal that the bishop had to have it covered with a veil."[6]

The process of symbolization of an abstract concept is a long and complicated one. Until the concept emerges as an anthropomorphic symbol, as in the case of Osiris or Buddha, it goes through several stages that seem to follow a distinct order. First there is the concept, symbolized by an abstract (aniconic) symbol. This in turn is symbolized by a zoomorphic one, and that eventually is combined with, associated with, or replaced by an anthropomorphic symbol.

Abstract symbols do not maintain their hold over the imagination of the people, who demand more concrete embodiments or personifications in their need to visualize an abstract concept.

Following are several examples tracing the transformation of symbols (we omit dendromorphic and other minor forms in order to emphasize the principle):

CONCEPT	ABSTRACT SYMBOL	THERIOMOR-PHIC or ZOOMORPHIC SYMBOL	ANTHROPO-MORPHIC SYMBOL
Holy Ghost	Golden rays	Dove	Third person of Trinity
Soul	Shadow or Breath	Butterfly, Bird	Winged youth
Divine power	Thunderbolt	Eagle	Zeus
Life	Flame	Panther, Lion, Ox, and Goat	Dionysus
Life	Ankh cross or moon	Cow	Isis
Sun God	Djed pillar	Bull	Osiris
God, the Preserver	Solar discus	Garuda	Vishnu
Timelessness	Circle	Snake biting its own tail	Buddha in Nirvana
Storm god	Axe	Bull	Adad
Great mother	Meteoric stone	Pair of Lions	Kybele

With certain symbols some of these stages may be omitted, as in the case of the concept of innocence, for which no abstract symbol is known, but whose zoomorphic symbol is the lamb, which also symbolizes Christ. In the instance of

the Logos, its abstract symbol is the Alpha and Omega, no zoomorphic
symbol is known (unless we take the Lion of Judah [Rev. 5:5] as its zoomorphic
symbol—but confusion arises from the fact that it applies to the second
person of the Trinity, who, according to the Nicene Creed, is consubstantial
with the first and third person), but its anthropomorphic ones are a hand
issuing from clouds or a rainbow and, later, an old bearded man. In the case of
visual symbols of abstract concepts, allegorism is the last stage of transformation
into figurative substitutions, until in some cases the original concept is lost.
An allegory is more of a literary device that substitutes for the anthropomorphic
symbol further, ever more remote imagery. Typical symbol sequences are:
Logos—cross—fish—bearded male—unicorn; sky father—keraunos—
eagle—bearded male—bull raping Europa; destructive principle—drum—bull—
dancing Shiva—infinite lingam.

The principle of the transformation of symbols can be tested in reverse.
Every allegorical scene covers up earlier, more abstract types of symbols.
For instance, in typical scenes of the Enlightenment of Buddha under the Bodhi
tree, protected by the *naga* (hooded serpent), there are present an anthropomorphic
symbol (the Buddha), a zoomorphic one (the serpent), and a dendromorphic
symbol (the Bodhi tree). All of these symbols replaced the more abstract
and earlier wheel of the law, throne, stupa, trisula, umbrella, mountain, and
so forth. In a discussion of the four gateways of the great Stupa at Sanchi
(Andhra Dynasty, c. first century B.C.), Sir John Marshall wrote:

> *Most of the inscriptions carved here and there on the gateways record,*
> *like those on the balustrades, the names of the pious individuals or*
> *guilds who contributed to their erection, or take the form of*
> *imprecatory curses on anyone so impious as to appropriate the*
> *gateways to the use of an unorthodox sect. Not one of them says a*
> *word, unfortunately, of the scenes and figures delineated, the*
> *interpretation of which is all the more difficult owing to the practice,*
> *universal in the Early School of Indian Art, of never portraying the*
> *Buddha in bodily form, but of indicating his presence merely by some*
> *symbol, such as his foot-prints or the throne on which he sat,*
> *or the sacred tree associated with his enlightenment.*[7]

A SIXFOLD SCHEMA OF SYMBOLISM

This principle applies to Mesopotamian, Egyptian, Hindu, Buddhist, Greek, Roman, and Christian art. One exception is prehistoric art, where the process was in some cases reversed, from figurization to abstract—possibly because of a simplification of outlines which, through timeless repetitions, became abstracted. It is possible that many Mezolithic and Neolithic symbols and signs were once zoomorphic or anthropomorphic. The arts of Judaism and Islam are also excluded because of the prohibitions against representations of men and animals, except in a decorative or illustrative sense. These two religions, with rare exceptions, developed only abstract, symbolic vocabularies.

There are still two kinds of symbols as yet neither recognized nor named by scholars; these, in conjunction with the known stages (abstract, zoomorphic, anthropomorphic, and allegoric), delineate the entire scale of human religious and aesthetic experience, from nonsymbolic to allegoric processes. The two kinds are 1) metasymbolic, or that style of modern art in which the forms, lines, and colors do not symbolize anything outside themselves, and 2) asymbolic, mystic identification with ultimate reality.

Several modern philosophers assert that all of our perceptions take place on a symbolic level, for the encounter with reality undergoes so many transformations that what we ultimately experience is not the reality itself but a symbol of it. However, in spite of the arguments of logicians, semanticists, and psychologists, there are at least two kinds of experience of reality which may be said to be nonsymbolic. One is the mystical experience, the other a certain kind of nonobjective art which may be called metasymbolic.[8]

We live in a time which has no vital tradition of symbolism, but we do not live in a time without creative art. Rebelling against all traditions, symbolic as well as stylistic, the abstract shows a way to a new awareness of the absolute. What traditional symbolism has lost in validity has been regained by the abstractionists in private imagery. The personal experience is the only experience that has validity; this has long been true in the field of religious experience as well as art.

Among the qualities which lend significance to the historical styles of art is the degree of their abstraction from nature. One style overcomes and spiritualizes the form with mysterious shadows, another with light. Certain styles distort, others perfect a heightened magic or *surrealism* which reveals the world anew—but there is always an attempt to abstract. Abstract or, more correctly, nonobjective art can be compared to a screen that filters out representational elements. This does not imply that representational styles cannot evoke a spiritual reality, but it is extremely difficult to transfigure the world of appearance. Nonobjectivism has hurdled all such barriers and penetrated beyond nature into the very heart of the energies and spiritual tensions of the cosmos.

Since the direct, visual translation of spiritual states of mind could not be realized before the advent of nonobjectivism, the earlier styles either had to disguise them, as Rembrandt did, with the use of his inner light, or suggest other dimensions by breaking up the apparent solidity of form, as in Cubism. Nonobjectivism in its purest state rejects all references to nature, objects, or symbolism and represents the first meaningful yet nonsymbolic style in the history of art. What it communicates lies hidden solely within its own formal world, which carries no associative or denotative values whatsoever. In the masterpieces of this style, which we have called metasymbolic, there is an indissoluble unity between energies, form, and meaning. Piet Mondrian's severe, mathematically perfect compositions transubstantiate line and right angles into pure spirit. Those who can understand the mysteries of his grid system can understand an aspect of the absolute.

Pure abstraction has been in existence for about 50 years. It was started by Kandinsky and Mondrian, each finding in it an avenue for personal expression. Both arrived at their respective styles out of spiritual necessities. To them the destruction of natural forms, traditional symbolism, and superficial imagery liberated the spirit. What they aimed at were eternal images removed from the accidental time-bound conformations of manifested nature. That the genesis of nonobjective art is due not to aesthetic considerations but primarily to spiritual ones is carefully documented in their published writings.[9]

Even if nonobjective art has entered its decline because of a movement to return to the figure and nature, any future criticism should give its due to the heroic attempt of many artists to transcend man and the visible world in favor of an absolute ideal. Nonobjective art, the aesthetics of the absolute, demonstrates the possibility of apprehending and expressing metaphysical concepts without recourse to symbols, language, or subject matter.

Plotinus, St. Augustine, Dionysius the Aeropagite, Erigena, Thomas à Kempis, Meister Eckhardt, St. John of the Cross, Jacob Boehme, George Fox, and many other Western mystics have experienced a direct encounter with the absolute which is, by definition, a nonsymbolic experience. Well-trained yogins, also, know that when they have achieved the highest state of meditation, identification with Brahma, they have risen beyond myths and symbols. The true yogin stills his mind to such a degree that all thought processes and all sense impressions cease to exist for the time being. As the Maitri Upanishad 6:24 puts it:

> But when the mind has been dissolved,
> And there is the joy whose only witness is the self—
> That is Brahma, the immortal, the pure!
> That is the way! That indeed is the world![10]

Dr. Mircea Eliade, the eminent historian of religion, has recently made the following assertion: "reality that is strictly metaphysical . . . can be approached in no other way than through myths and symbols."[11] The limitations raised by Dr. Eliade have been refuted countless times by mystics, both Christian and non-Christian, who have achieved mergence into ultimate reality. The classic Christian instance is the saying, "I and the Father are one." (John 10:30). This was spoken *viva voce* in Aramaic to the Jews in the temple in the portico of Solomon in an historical situation. Significantly enough, Dionysius the Aeropagite quoted this saying in his famous mystical treatise *The Divine Names*, Chapter II.[12]

St. Augustine and Dionysius have set the pattern for the mystic ascent in Christian terms. Most important later mystics have taken their inspiration from one or the other. St. Augustine describes in his *Confessions* (IX:25) how every activity, physical and mental, and every sound and symbol must be "silenced" in quest of identification with the absolute.

Suppose, for any person, that the tumult of the flesh be silenced—

> silenced, the images of earth and water and air; silenced, the very
> heavens; silenced, his very soul unto himself, then, if he pass
> beyond himself, ceasing to think of himself by means of images—
> silenced, his dreams and imaginary apparitions, every tongue
> and every sign [i.e., symbol] and whatever comes to be by transition,
> if he be granted this complete silence . . . and if, having said this,
> they become quiet, once they have lifted up their ear to Him who made
> them; then, if He alone speak, not through them, but through
> Himself, so that we might hear His Word, not through fleshly speech,
> or through the voice of an angel, or through the crash of thunder,
> or through the darkness of a similitude, but Himself whom we
> love in these things, just as now we reached out and, with the speed
> of thought, touched the Eternal Wisdom abiding above all things—
> and if this could continue, and other visions of a much lower type
> were taken away, and this one vision were to enrapture, absorb
> and enclose its beholder in inner joys, so that life might forever be
> like that instant of understanding, for which we have sighed, then
> surely, this is the meaning of: "Enter into the joy of Thy Master"?[13]

Dionysius the Aeropagite, who, like St. Augustine, belongs to the Neo-Platonic tradition, makes the conditions for mystic union even clearer and insists that the seeker must renounce "all the apprehensions of his understanding," which, as a matter of course, include myths, symbols, and language.

> . . . let us set before our minds the scriptural rule that in speaking about
> God we should declare the Truth, not with enticing words of man's
> wisdom, but in demonstration of the power which the Spirit stirred
> up in the Sacred Writers, whereby, in a manner surpassing speech
> and knowledge, we embrace those truths which, in like manner surpass
> them, in that Union which exceeds our faculty, and exercise of
> discursive, and of intuitive reason.[14]

In another place he states the paradox of mysticism, that one must renounce all knowledge in order to rise to absolute knowledge.

> *. . . the divinest and highest of the things perceived by the eyes of the body*
> *or the mind are but the symbolic language of things subordinate*
> *to Him who Himself transcendeth them all. Through these things*
> *His incomprehensible presence is shown walking upon those heights*
> *of His holy places which are perceived by the mind; and when it*
> *breaks forth, even from the things that are beheld and from those*
> *that behold them, and plunges the true initiate unto the Darkness*
> *of Unknowing wherein he renounces all the apprehensions of*
> *his understanding and is enwrapped in that which is wholly intangible*
> *and invisible, belonging wholly to Him that is beyond all things and*
> *to none else (whether himself or another), and being through the*
> *passive stillness of all his reasoning powers united by his highest*
> *faculty to Him that is wholly unknowable, of whom thus by a*
> *rejection of all knowledge he possesses a knowledge that exceeds*
> *his understanding.*[15]

The consensus of all mystics is that ultimate reality *can* be experienced on an asymbolic level of absorption, merger, union, or identification. But when a mystic wants to speak of it, he is forced to use a symbolic system like language or, in Plotinus' words, "the image" (Enneads V:3,6). To assert, however, that without myths and symbols the absolute cannot be apprehended contradicts, without evidence to the contrary, the long tradition of Christian and non-Christian mysticism. "The philosopher Isidorus (5th Cent. A.D.) we are told in the fragments of the life of him written by Damascius, 'did not care to offer homage to images; he went to the gods themselves direct, the gods who are hidden, not in the holy places of temples, but hidden within the soul, in the inexpressible region, whatever it may be, of nescience (*agnosia*). How then did he go to the gods such as these? He went by a kind of mighty love, itself inexpressible. What we mean by this love those who have experience of it know, but to say what it is in words is impossible, even to conceive of it in thought is not any easier.' "[16]

Those who call for a return to symbolism, including theologians concerned with the liturgical revival, rarely, if ever, suggest which of the wealth of traditional symbols they would like to see revived. Do any of these still have the power to teach, shock, or convert us? Let us look at one symbol, the fish, and one myth, the unicorn.

The fish has been a popular magical amulet, a symbol of life and fertility, as well as an astrological sign, since pre-Babylonian times. One of the most ancient gods of the Mesopotamian plain, Ea, god of water and wisdom, was represented by a composite symbol, an ibex and fish. From Mesopotamia this symbol diffused over most of the ancient world. In India it became the symbol of Vishnu's first incarnation (*matsya*); in this form, as divine fish, he saved Manu, the first man, from the flood. The Buddhists included the fish as one of their eight auspicious symbols. In the West the fish was associated primarily with female goddesses. The Egyptians, for instance, worshiped the oxyrynchus fish as sacred to Isis, Hathor, Nut, and other goddesses. According to Ovid, Venus transformed herself into a fish. Derceto (or Atargatis) was a goddess of Hieropolis, in Syria; fish were sacred to her because she was believed to have either fallen into a lake and been saved by a fish or transformed into one. She was therefore depicted as half-woman, half-fish. Eros, god of love, the child of Aphrodite, is represented in classic art as riding upon a dolphin (confused in classic times with a fish). In this manner various symbols were combined in one image—the creative sea, the fish symbol itself, and the divine child.

The fish became a secret sign of recognition among Christians during the period of their persecution. Clement of Alexandria permitted its use on seal rings, and Tertullian enlarged its meaning to include baptism: "But we, little fishes, after the example of OUR FISH Jesus Christ, are born in water."[17] About three centuries later, St. Augustine said that in the word *fish* "Christ is mystically understood, because he was able to live, that is, to exist, without sin in the abyss of mortality as in the depth of waters."[18] He was undoubtedly referring to the famous acrostic *Ichthys*, which yielded, in Greek, the sentence, "Jesus Christ Son of God, Savior."

There is still no agreement among scholars which particular instance in the New Testament gave the Fathers the authority to call Christ "fish," nor why the Eucharist was symbolized by a fish, as in Roman catacomb paintings and on many early Christian sarcophagi (Fig. 33). An early third-century inscription

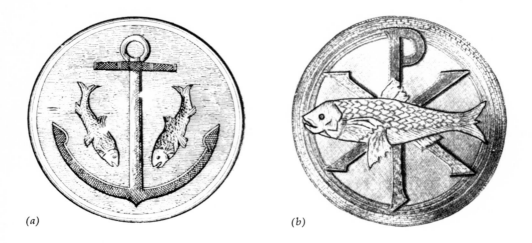

(a)

(b)

by Abercius, Bishop of Hieropolis in Phrygia (recognized, however, as pagan by several scholars, such as Robert Eisler and Albrecht Dieterich), is still cited as historical support for the fish as a symbol of Christ. The important point is that at no time did Christ refer to himself as a fish or a fisherman. Peter, as we know, is connected with fish, both professionally as well as symbolically (Mark 1:17). The feeding of the multitudes (Mark 6:35–44) gives no direct support to this symbol, nor does Christ's partaking of broiled fish after the Resurrection (Luke 24:42–43). There is nothing in the account of the miraculous drought in Lake Gennesaret which convincingly suggests the fish as a symbol of Christ (Luke 5:4–9). The feeding of the disciples with bread and fish after the Resurrection (John 21:9–14) has traditionally been connected with the Eucharist. But in New Testament context itself the fish is not a Eucharistic symbol, and there is no compelling reason to interpret the above passage as such. The Last Supper, it will be remembered, consisted only of bread and wine (Mark 14:22–25).

In one instance, Christ mentioned the "sign of Jonah" (Matt. 12:39) as referring to himself. "For as Jonah became a sign to the men of Nineveh, so will the Son of man be to this generation" (Luke 11:30). His three days in the belly of the fish were compared by Christ to the three days which he spent

in the "heart of the earth" (Matt. 12:40). But even in this instance the fish
neither symbolizes Jonah nor Christ, who is "greater than Jonah" (Matt. 12:41).
The parable of the fish net (Matt. 13:47) and the story of the shekel in the fish's
mouth (Matt. 17:27) are too indirect to have any bearing upon the symbol
(of Christ) under discussion. Jeremiah's "many fishers" (Jer. 16:16) applies
to the scourge of Israel, and other, even more oblique references to fish
hooks (Amos 4:2) or fish nets (Hab. 1:14–17) either are not complimentary
to Israel or refer to its enemies. Even if forced into allegorical interpretations,
these instances would lend no support to the fish as a symbol of Christ,
although they admit, of course, as do some of the above references, of other
allegories. This exhausts the scriptural possibilities, except for Leviathan, a
gigantic fish monster who was destroyed by the Lord (Isa. 27:1). The Christian
fish symbol, therefore, must be considered an accretion that cannot be
explained logically as having grown out of scriptural soil.

Erwin R. Goodenough has recently demonstrated conclusively that the fish
is an ancient, extremely diffused symbol of life and immortality that was
adopted even by the Jews in the decoration of synagogues (Dura), catacombs,
and amulets.[19] This symbol constituted a *lingua franca* in the Graeco-Roman
world and was borrowed freely by nearly all the religions of that time.
"Christianity and Judaism alike rejected Dionysus and his rites and myths with
horror, while they kept his symbols." Elsewhere in his monumental study,
Goodenough states that "the Jews themselves seem to me to have been
enriching the fish symbol with *ex post facto* interpretation when in later writings
they joined it with the zodiacal Pisces, in ascendance in the month of Adar,
the last month of the Jewish year and so, they said, the symbol of the last age,
that of the Messiah."[20]

The fish symbol was incorporated into Christian allegorical thinking during
the postapostolic period, for it was a popular symbol which could easily be
joined to certain Old and New Testament statements. The Jews of the
dispersion had already accepted it as a messianic symbol (according to postexilic
rabbinical legends, the great fish Leviathan would be sacrificed during the

34   The Hunt of the Unicorn, French
     Tapestry (Late XV Century). The
     Cloisters Collection, Gift of J. D.
     Rockefeller, Jr., 1937, Courtesy The
     Metropolitan Museum of Art, New
     York

messianic age) in spite of the ancient prohibitions in Deuteronomy 4:18, which, at least until the period of kings, applied to its symbolic usage as well.[21] In Old Testament context the fish is still an inferior creature subject to Adam (Gen. 1:26) and fearful of Noah (Gen. 9:2). Men, like fish, are victims of cruel fate (Eccles. 9:12), and fish fear the presence of God (Ezra 38:20). In short, the fish as a sacred Christian symbol must have come from other than Old Testament sources. Indeed, Goodenough's conclusion is that Jews and Christians alike borrowed their symbols, of which the fish is one, from a common pagan (Dionysiac) source.

The fish, in addition to symbolizing Christ, is also used as a symbol of baptism, of the faithful, and of the Eucharist. Although ingestion or prohibition of certain sacred foods accompanies many religions, the traditional custom of eating fish on Friday in Latin cultures seems like a substitute, if not a rival, Eucharist.

The fish symbol has been used in Christianity for almost 2,000 years, and in non-Christian religions for about five millennia. It is inadequate as a symbol for Christ, and its significance is ambiguous.

The unicorn is more complex than the fish symbol, for it is a myth, an allegory, and a symbol all at once. It was one of the favorite images of Christ during the Age of Faith (Fig. 34). So-called unicorn horns were kept and exhibited in many churches and were regarded as sacred objects worthy of devotion. The church of St. Denis, near Paris, boasted a seven-foot-long specimen. St. Mark's, in Venice, exhibited two horns which had been looted in Constantinople, one of which was inscribed on its silver handle, "John Palaeologus, Emperor, Unicorn good against poison." The Cathedral of Milan and Westminster Abbey kept large specimens, and many other less wealthy

churches had fragments of this miraculous material. There was no royal
treasury or wealthy prince who did not have one. A section of a "true unicorn's
horn" (*verum cornu monocerotis*) was worth over ten times its weight in
gold; entire horns sometimes brought twice that much.

This popularity is ascribable in part to the then universal belief that the
horn itself, or beakers made of it, could detect the presence of poison. Even
leading thinkers of the Middle Ages, such as Hildegarde of Bingen, Albertus
Magnus, and Peter Albano, were convinced of this. Beakers of this miraculous
material were used at the tables of those who could afford them, undoubtedly
because of the widespread fear of being poisoned. This particular aspect
of the unicorn myth can be traced to India.

The Greek physician Ctetsias, who was employed during the fifth century B.C. at
the court of the Persian king Darius II, wrote the first account of this myth. In
a lost book of his, *Indica*, preserved in an abstract by the ninth-century Greek
philosopher and churchman Photius, we find the following description of
the unicorn, substantially the same as was circulated during the Middle Ages, by
which time it had already become a symbol as well as an allegory of Christ.

> There are in India certain wild asses which are as large as horses, and
> larger. Their bodies are white, their heads dark red and their eyes
> dark blue. They have a horn on the forehead which is about a foot and
> half in length. The dust filed from this horn is administered in a potion
> as a protection against deadly drugs. The base of this horn, for two
> hands breadth above the brow, is pure white; the upper part is sharp
> and of a vivid crimson . . . and the remainder, or middle portion is
> black. Those who drink out of these horns, made into drinking vessels,
> are not subject, they say, to convulsions or to the holy disease
> [epilepsy]. Indeed, they are immune even to poisons if, either before

or after swallowing such, they drink wine, water or anything else
from these beakers. . . . The animal is exceedingly swift and powerful,
so that no creature, neither the horse nor any other, can overtake it.[22]

In this description can be found the origin of the theory of the curative effects of
the unicorn horn and of the animal's capacity to elude would-be captors.

The other, better known aspect of the unicorn myth, the "Virgin Capture,"
undoubtedly derives from an independent tradition, perhaps Arabic or Chinese.
It is the latter version, popularized by the Bestiaries, which we find represented
in so many manuscripts, tapestries, stained glass windows, and vessels of the
High Middle Ages (Fig. 35). One Bestiary (Physiologus) asserts: "He is a small
animal, like a kid, but surprisingly fierce for his size, with one very sharp horn

on his head, and no hunter is able to capture him by force. Yet there is a trick by which he is taken. Men lead a virgin to the place where he most resorts and leave her there alone. As soon as he sees this virgin he runs and lays his head in her lap. She fondles him and he falls asleep. The hunters then approach and capture him and lead him to the palace of the king."[23] Other sources assert that the unicorn is attracted by the "odour of virginity" and can also be employed to test the chastity of young girls.

A Syriac version of the Bestiary gives the following, somewhat more erotic variant:

> There is an animal called dajja, extremely gentle, which the hunters are unable to capture because of its great strength. It has in the middle of its brow a single horn. But observe the ruse by which the huntsmen take it. They lead forth a young virgin, pure and chaste, to whom, when the animal sees her, he approaches, throwing himself upon her. Then the girl offers him her breasts, and the animal begins to suck the breasts of the maiden and to conduct himself freely with her. Then the girl, while sitting quietly, reaches forth her hand and grasps the horn on the animals brow, and at this point the huntsmen come up and take the beast and go away with him to the king.—Likewise the Lord Christ has raised up for us a horn of salvation in the midst of Jerusalem, in the house of God, by the intercession of the mother of God, a virgin pure, chaste, full of mercy, immaculate, inviolate.[24]

Elusiveness, eroticism, poison protection, and virgin capture became fused and confused, assuring this myth great popularity in the medieval mind. In the Chinese version, in spite of the more pronounced phallic elements, there are undeniable typological connections with the West. Chinese writers themselves say that the unicorn, or Ki-lin, is not native to China, but that it comes from "afar." A Ki-lin is supposed to have appeared to the mother of Confucius just before his birth, holding in its mouth a jade tablet bearing an inscription which declared her son's future greatness. Pictures of the Ki-lin were used in women's quarters of Chinese homes as charms to promote the birth of great men or, at least, of boys rather than girls.[25]

A SIXFOLD SCHEMA OF SYMBOLISM

The unicorn myth persisted until about the seventeenth century, when so-called unicorn horns were finally recognized as narwhale tusks brought to the European market by increased whale-hunting activities in the far North. Before that time Islamic traders sold them without divulging their sources, contributing to their alleged mysterious origin. The narwhale tusk is not a horn, but an elongated, pointed and twisted, left canine tooth of the male. This realization of a more scientific age dealt the final blow to this myth.

The very fact that the unicorn myth has ingloriously died as an allegory of Christ proves that it could not sustain its claims to make possible an apprehension of the absolute. Ideally the purpose of symbols is to simplify and convey complex abstract concepts, but they can also distort and misrepresent. Whatever will emerge by way of a future religious symbolism, one thing is certain—one cannot catch the absolute in a unicorn or a fish.

It is the nature of the human mind to personify and to assign attributes to abstract concepts. As we have seen above, the symbolic process becomes increasingly removed from the fundamental concept as it goes in turn through its zoomorphic, anthropomorphic, and allegorical stages. This process obeys predictable behavior.

There is a hierarchy of symbols consisting of six stages, which range from asymbolism to allegorism. In this hierarchy the so-called abstract symbol does not occupy the highest place but is preceded by two higher stages and succeeded by three stages of relative decline.

ASYMBOLIC (Mystic experience)

Nonsymbolic, nonverbal encounter with ultimate reality

METASYMBOLIC (Nonobjective art or analogous forms)

Nondenotative, nonconnotative, self-referrent; form and meaning fused

---

SYMBOLIC ABSTRACT (Aniconic patterns)

Connotative of larger, abstract concepts

A SIXFOLD SCHEMA OF SYMBOLISM

ZOOMORPHIC, THERIOMORPHIC, ICHTHYOMORPHIC

(Representations of animals, birds, and fish) Once removed from the abstract symbol; concretization of attributes and qualities

---

ANTHROPOMORPHIC *(Human ideal types)*

Twice removed from the abstract symbol; personification of an abstract concept

---

ALLEGORIC *(Figurative substitutes, disguised symbolism)*

Thrice removed from the abstract symbol; narrative, moralizing, popular imagery; also hidden esoteric message

---

Growing out of this is the following principle: Each successive stage of symbolization after the third entails a progressive weakening of the concept until the sixth stage is reached, in which it is lost.

The Eclipse of Symbolism

SYMBOLS DESIGNATE NOT CAUSAL but analogous relationships, magical connections, so-called correspondences between the chosen or created symbols and the powers of nature. They concatenate man, his symbols, and natural phenomena into a vast theoretical system. Visual religious and art symbols always start with concrete realities. Ancient man was extremely observant, as the anatomical details of the pregnant fertility figurines of the Paleolithic period demonstrate. Yet causal relationships obviously eluded him, as the figurines were expected to promote the birth of children on the theory that "like influences (or produces) like." Formal aspects of symbols were always based upon empirical observations and were carefully delineated, as in the prehistoric animals in the French and Spanish caves, Egyptian animal deities, flower and astronomical symbols, and anthropomorphic gods. Even grotesque demons were based upon observations of human deformities and imaginative exaggerations of important details such as eyes, feet, hands, breasts, gestures, and so forth. So-called abstract symbols as well, although they belong to a different class, derive in the main from more naturalistic ones, which have become abstracted through timeless repetition.

THE ECLIPSE OF SYMBOLISM

Symbols possess a formal and a theoretical aspect. Although their formal aspects are based upon empirical observation (regardless of how stylized), their theoretical aspects are based upon various assumptions—the theory of correspondence, i.e., the microcosm reflects the macrocosm, like influences like; consecrated images are the focus; of active powers that can defend, heal, or destroy. It was believed widely up until about the seventeenth century that stars and planets possessed souls, that their course and positions in respect to each other would affect the destinies and organs of man, that mountain tops were the natural gathering places for demons or gods, that earthquakes and atmospheric or celestial disturbances were the gods' warnings to man, that menstruating women would adversely affect growing plants, that diseases were punishments for sins, that touching hunchbacks brought luck, that some statues of the gods possessed healing powers, that certain symbols scared demons away and others attracted benevolent powers, and so forth. Practically every object and animal known to ancient man played a role in magical practices or rituals and thus served its turn as a symbol.[1]

Belief in symbols requires a priori judgments not dependent upon experience, tests, or failure. Once a symbol was accepted as such by a group, its efficacy was not doubted and its powers were not tested. The symbol never failed in the eyes of the believer, and therefore there was no need to test it—that is, to take the first step that would have led to science. As Bronislaw Malinowski has put it, "Magic is thus not derived from an observation of nature or knowledge of its laws, it is a primeval possession of man to be known only through tradition and affirming man's autonomous power of creating desired ends.... It is thus never conceived as a force of nature, residing in things, acting independently of man, to be found out and learned by him, by any of those proceedings by which he gains his ordinary knowledge of nature."[2] If a symbol, such as the magic pentagram of medieval practices, failed to do its work, the magician would have believed that he had not executed all the steps of his ritual correctly. He would not have drawn the conclusion that because the pentagram failed all such symbols are powerless. Failure of a symbol to produce an effect was not ascribed to the symbol itself, but either to lack of faith in its powers or to incorrect ritual and application.

THE ECLIPSE OF SYMBOLISM

The eclipse of symbolism has its own inner logic, which will be sketched below.
Symbolism, the employment of, belief in, and reliance upon symbols,
has run its course; its alleged mediating powers between man and the cosmos
have been recognized as fallacious.

The belief in the efficacy of symbols and the theory of correspondence
may be called the symbolic fallacy. Symbols may stand for what they signify,
such as wavy lines, which are an iconic symbol for water; or they may be unlike
what they signify, such as the cow of Isis, or the eagle of Zeus; or they may
be so far removed from the concept or phenomenon that any connection between
them is obscured, as in an allegory. The symbolic fallacy may be traced to
the Paleolithic belief that everything and anything was symbolic. When the
success of all activity, from the hunt to procreation, depended upon magic
(as human procreation was contingent upon the presence of pregnant fertility
images), then life may be said to have functioned on a pansymbolic level.
Géza Róheim reports a personal observation which helps us to visualize
the extent to which symbolical, that is magical, thinking permeated primitive
societies.

> One of my native friends of Normanby Island once gave me an incantation
> for killing crocodiles. (It was, he felt, a very effective incantation.)
> Then he described how he killed the crocodile with an axe. He had
> both the faith that he could do it (a knowledge of the incantation)
> and the necessary tools. Without magic, the natives said, we could
> do nothing at all: we could not till the soil, make love or war,
> navigate the sea, or do anything else.[3]

Paleolithic man was not aware of causal relationships, and he had little freedom
to act. He existed somewhat as a furtive intruder in a totally alien and magic
world which he tried, to a small extent, to manipulate through symbols
and rituals.

The concept of the Sacred and the Profane, which originated during the
Neolithic period, marked the beginning of the progressive desymbolization of
the world. Dr. Mircea Eliade recently commented upon this important
division, without which society could not have organized its various functions.

"For all history is in some measure a fall of the sacred, a limitation and diminution."[4] If everything were sacred, a well-developed society could not function. There is a rhythm between the Sacred and the Profane, as there is between silence and speech, sleeping and walking. To regret that everything is not sacred is to reject those activities and everyday necessities which cannot be sacred in themselves. And without the existence of a recognized profane realm, the sacred one would lose most of its significance. It is true that profane activities may serve an ultimate end which is sacred, but one cannot read an ethical character into the activities of Neolithic man. Through the discovery of the significance of the profane realm, he tamed the sacred one, which was always synonymous with the uncanny, the demonic, and the dangerous. "With few exceptions, modern anthropologists agree that primitive man, like civilized man, lives in two worlds, the matter-of-fact workaday world and the magico-religious world, and that he employs various psychic and social devices for keeping them separate. Primitive man is sometimes rational and practical [operating in the profane realm], sometimes irrational and superstitious [when entering the sacred realm]. He has two principles of causation: the natural and, what may rather vaguely be called the supernatural."[5]

The separation of the temple, or sacred area, from the everyday world focused the mysterious powers in an exclusive precinct (*temenos*) with exclusive functions. Man became aware of some causal relationships, such as seeding and harvesting, cross-breeding, and so forth, and through these practices he gained confidence in his own powers to achieve certain goals without complete reliance upon symbols, the *sine qua non* of magic and ritual. As the profane realm grew in importance, the sacred realm contracted into the temple, the palace (sacred kinship), and specific rituals. Thus the Paleolithic "pansymbolic" interpretation of the world became a partially symbolic one during the Neolithic period. Questioning the symbolic quality of one aspect of nature opens the way to questioning all symbols.

The discovery of the objective character of symbols as formal rather than psychic configurations destroys their so-called magic aura. However, one may lose faith in one symbol and retain it in another, or, what is more common, one may reject those of another religion or culture in favor of one's own.

THE ECLIPSE OF SYMBOLISM

The ancient Hebrews vigorously attacked the images of the pagans, yet they treasured teraphim at home and cherubim in the temple of Solomon, and they slid back into worship of the golden calf, high places, and other symbols.

In spite of the inconsistencies of the ancient Hebrews, they did not have a pansymbolic world view, but they were able, several centuries before the Greek Skeptics, to regard symbols objectively as formal configurations. "Woe to him who says to a wooden thing, Awake; to a dumb stone, Arise! Can this give revelation? Behold, it is overlaid with gold and silver, and there is no breath at all in it." (Hab. 2:19). Many philosophers and mystics after the Hebrews rejected symbols and the theory of correspondence. Clement of Alexandria put it very clearly: "I seek after God not the works of God."[6] St. Paul wrote, in his First Letter to the Corinthians (8:4), "an idol has no real existence." Evidently he did not want to be drawn into arguments on the so-called occult relationship of matter and spirit, the alleged psychic powers of symbols, or the theory of consecrated images, but dismissed the whole problem with one stroke. In a more philosophical vein, Antisthenes, the disciple of Socrates, said: "God is not like to any; wherefore no one can know him from an image."[7] "According to Photius, Aenesidemus held that invisible things cannot be revealed by visible things, and a belief in such things is an illusion. . . ."[8]

Clement of Alexandria, with a remarkably scientific cast of mind, rejected those symbols of the gods which he recognized as simple celestial phenomena.

> *As the Halo is not a god, and as the Iris [rainbow] is not a god, but are states of the atmosphere and of the clouds; and as, likewise, a day is not a god, nor a year, not time, which is made up of these, so neither is sun nor moon, by which each of those mentioned above is determined. . . . Still further, if the lightnings, and thunderbolts, and rains are not gods, how can fire and water be gods? How can shooting stars and comets, which are produced by atmospheric changes?*[9]

Belief in symbols, so vigorously attacked by the Hebrew prophets and by certain leading Hellenistic philosophers, was also rejected by nascent Christianity. Until the fourth century the church discouraged visual images and looked upon symbols with suspicion. Plato's pansymbolic world view, as expressed in the Timaeus and elsewhere, ultimately prevailed, however, sweeping away all opposition to symbols and images.

That the medieval concept of life was allegorical and that the fantastic replaced the real needs no proof or elaboration. The inordinate preference for symbols, from the unicorn to the alchemists' elixirs, led down a path from which there was no return until the very basis of symbolism and allegorism was questioned by isolated philosophers, reformers, and scientists. The orientation of medieval society was toward pansymbolism, in which everything, including scientific errors, was believed to mirror a divine pattern. As St. Bonaventure put it, in *The Mind's Road to God* (thirteenth century): "the world is itself a ladder for ascending to God. . . . But since with respect to the mirror of sensible things it happens that God is contemplated not only *through* them, as by His traces, but also *in* them, insofar as He is in them by essence, potency and presence. . . ."[10] The medieval world acquired a dissimulated character seen through successive veils of symbols which replaced reality and, in the minds of many, became its substitute. From this it follows that those who saw the world in symbolic terms did not see it at all. The desymbolization of the world is due to scientists who took natural phenomena away from the Doctors and allegorists and subjected them to rational analysis.

The process which characterizes the gradual change from a symbolic world view to the scientific, experimental method can be expressed by a theorem: There is a reduction of the symbolic content of any phenomenon in inverse proportion to its descriptive or analytical interpretation. Astrology, for instance, was an entirely symbolic system, and therefore entirely false. Medieval cosmology (upon which medieval philosophy depended) was also entirely false, because it was based upon two errors: 1) a scientific one, the belief that the earth is in the center of the universe, and 2) a symbolic one, the belief that the universe was therefore created for man. Alchemy, on the other hand, was a partially symbolic and partially experimental system. That part which concerned itself with the symbolism of alchemy and the finding of the philosopher's stone was false, while its experimental aspects contributed to the development of chemistry. The gradual desymbolization of the world and of the cosmos led to more and more direct confrontations with nature, and thus to basic, scientific discoveries. But the way in which the vestiges of a symbolic interpretation of phenomena can lead even a great scientist into error can be demonstrated by Copernicus' discovery.

He wrote, in his *De Revolutionibus Orbium Celestium* (1543), Book I:

> *First of all we assert that the universe is spherical; partly because this form, being a complete whole, needing no joints, is the most perfect of all; partly because it constitutes the most spacious form, which is thus best suited to contain and retain all things. . . . (Chapter I)*

> *Hereupon, we note that the motions of the heavenly bodies are circular. When a sphere is in motion it rotates, expressing, through this activity, its form as that of the simplest of bodies, in which there is to be found neither a beginning nor end; nor can the beginning be distinguished from the end, as the sphere achieves, through the same intermediate points, its original position. (Chapter IV)*[11]

Copernicus disproved Aristotle's opinion (De Caelo, II: 13, 14) and, by implication, Plato's (Phaedo 108–109A), that the earth is located in the center of the universe (Book I, Chapters 7–8), but he held steadfastly, mainly for symbolic reasons, to the idea of the circular orbit of the "stars." In Book I, Chapter V, he mentioned that he had studied the Pythagorean and Platonic hypotheses of circular motion, and in Book I, Chapter X, he finally referred to the Timaeus of Plato. According to Plato:

> *Such was the mind and thought of god in the creation of time. The sun and moon and five other stars, which are called the planets, were created by him in order to distinguish and preserve the numbers of time: and when he had made their several bodies, he placed them in the orbits in which the circle of the other was revolving,—in seven orbits seven stars. (Timaeus 38; cf. 34, 36)*

> *. . . that other doctrine about the wandering of the sun and the moon and the other stars is not the truth, but the very reverse of the truth. Each of them moves in the same path—not in many paths, but in one only, which is circular. . . . (Laws, 822)*

THE ECLIPSE OF SYMBOLISM

We have a first-hand account that Copernicus was influenced by the Greek philosophers. George Joachim Rheticus, a student of Copernicus who lived with him for over two years, wrote in a letter to John Schöner, the *Narratio Prima*: "Following Plato and the Pythagoreans, the greatest mathematicians of that divine age, my teacher thought that in order to determine the causes of the phenomena circular motions must be ascribed to the spherical earth. . . ."[12]

Plato's image of the universe was that of an armillary sphere in which the motions of the outermost sphere and of the planets are represented by rings. Because the circle was to Plato the perfect symbol of the creating god, the animated stars (Timaeus 39, 41) must move in perfect circles. Copernicus did not free himself of Plato's symbolic interpretation of the circle; he did not search further, which might have led him toward the discovery of the elliptical orbit. But he did discover a scientific truth—that the earth is not in the center of the universe but moves as a planet among planets. Copernicus proceeded partially by observation and partially by symbolism, and it was the latter which led him astray.

A symbolic world view of any degree is synonymous with a magic world view. Such a view necessitates belief in the numinous content of nature, in the idea that nature reflects patterns, designs, or purposes of a higher origin, as formulated by the theory of correspondence. The Copernican error was based precisely upon this theory as it pertained to the circle. The destruction of the symbolic world view was accomplished gradually, with the Neolithic separation of the world into the Sacred and the Profane, the Hebrew prophets' attacks upon the alleged powers of symbols, criticism by certain Christian philosophers such as Clement of Alexandria, and philosophical schools such as Skepticism and Nominalism, culminating in the experimental scientific method. Following the lead of science, the vestiges of symbolic interpretations of phenomena will yield to descriptive and analytical techniques in all fields. One may assert, therefore, that insofar as any symbolic elements are part of the study, description, or observation of phenomena, those parts, and any conclusions based thereon, will be false.

Notes

Art Motifs as Symbols of Life and Society

1. Charles P. Mountford, "The Artist and His Art in an Australian Aboriginal Society" in *The Artist in Tribal Society*, ed. M. W. Smith (New York, 1961), pp. 14, 22.

2. *The Collected Dialogues of Plato*, ed. Edith Hamilton and Huntington Cairns (New York, 1961), pp. 1253–54.

3. The bas-relief from Laussel of a mutilated male torso and the reindeer horn engraving of a male figure among horses' heads, a serpent, and signs from La Madelaine (Dordogne) do not clearly indicate whether they represent hunters or are a new motif.

4. E. A. Wallis Budge, *The Book of the Opening of the Mouth* (London, 1909).

5. Henry Frankfort, *Kingship and the Gods* (Chicago, 1948), pp. 176–77.

6. E. A. Wallis Budge, *The Mummy* (Cambridge, Eng., 1925), p. 428.

7. John R. Spencer, trans. (New Haven, 1956), Book II, p. 67.

8. *The Destiny of Man* (London, 1954), p. 136.

9. *Art Journal*, XXII, No. 3, p. 182.

The Craft of Creation

1. Jowett, trans., p. 9.

2. Henry F. Osborne, *Men of the*

NOTES

Old Stone Age (New York, 1948),
pp. 358–423.

3. M. E. L. Mallowan, "IRAQ," II, I,
p. 105; cf. V. Gordon Childe, *New
Light on the Most Ancient East* (New
York, 1953), pp. 129, 216, 233, 234.

4. Christopher Dawson, *A Classical
Dictionary of Hindu Mythology and
Religion* (London, 1879), pp. 363–64, 129.

5. *Thespis* (New York, 1950), p. x.

6. The Hebrew word for "ground,"
adamah, is the feminine form of the
word for "man," *Adam*. James G. Frazer,
Folklore in the Old Testament
(London, 1919), I, 6.

7. T. Jacobsen, *The Intellectual
Adventure of Ancient Man*, ed. H.
Frankfort (Chicago, 1948), pp. 137, 145.

8. V. Gordon Childe, *Social Evolution*
(New York, 1951), pp. 23, 63, 151.

9. *What Happened in History*
(Harmondsworth, Middlesex, 1948), p. 85.

10. *Jewish Encyclopedia*, I, 208–10.

11. *Ibid.*, XII, p. 108.

12. Alexander Heidel, *The Gilgamesh
Epic and Old Testament Parallels*
(Chicago, 1949), pp. 2, 3, 14.

13. *Ibid.*, pp. 18, 19, 11, 33, 34.

14. Alexander Heidel, *The Babylonian
Genesis* (Chicago, 1951), pp. 66–67, 11,
18–27. Emphasis mine.

15. Ovid, *Metamorphoses* (Loeb
Classical Library), I, 400–10.

16. Gustave Glotz, *The Aegean
Civilization* (New York, 1925), p. 34.

17. *The Gods of the Egyptians* (London,
1904), II, 49–50.

18. Henry Frankfort, *Kingship and
the Gods* (Chicago, 1948), p. 148.

19. Henry Frankfort, *Ancient Egyptian
Religion* (New York, 1949), p. 20.

20. *Icon and Idea* (Cambridge,
1955), p. 59.

The Eye of God

1. S.A.B. Mercer, *The Pyramid
Texts* (New York, 1952), VI, 174.

2. Cf. F. Cumont, *The Mysteries of
Mithra* (Chicago, 1910).

3. R. E. Hume, *The Thirteen Principle
Upanishads* (Madras, 1949), p. 294.

4. *Ibid.*, p. 215.

5. *Ibid.*, p. 233.

6. Nonnus, *Dionysiaca* VII (Loeb
Classical Library, I), pp. 259, 261.

7. *Metamorphosis II* (Loeb Classical
Library, I), p. 63.

8. *Ibid.*, I, pp. 47, 51.

9. A. K. Gordon, *Tibetan Religious
Art* (New York, 1952), p. 44, Plate 45.

10. J. Harrison, *Prolegomena to the
Study of Greek Religion* (Cambridge,
1922), pp. 191–97.

11. *The Golden Bough*, Abridged ed.
(New York, 1947), p. 11.

12. H. Frankfort, *Ancient Egyptian
Religion* (New York, 1949), p. 24.

13. M. Bieber, *The Sculpture of the
Hellenistic Age* (New York, 1955), p. 167.

14. Max E. L. Mallowan, "Revelations
of Brilliant Art in North-East Syria
Over 4000 Years Ago," *Illustrated London*

News, October 15, 1938, pp. 697–701.

15. A. Castiglione, *Adventures of the Mind* (New York, 1946), p. 171.

16. Henry Nettleship and John E. Sandys, *A Dictionary of Classical Antiquities* (London, 1894), pp. 101, 234.

17. R. C. Thompson, *Semitic Magic* (London, 1908), p. 88.

18. A. Getty, *The Gods of Northern Buddhism* (Oxford, 1928), p. 198.

19. Hume, *op. cit.*, p. 262.

20. E. B. Havell, *The Ideals of Indian Art* (London, 1911), p. 51; J. Dowson, *A Classical Dictionary of Hindu Mythology* (London, 1879), p. 146.

21. Sir M. Monier-Williams, *A Sanskrit-English Dictionary* (Oxford, 1899), p. 221.

22. G. G. Coulton, *Medieval Panorama* (New York, 1944), p. 114.

23. Y. Hirn, *The Sacred Shrine* (London, 1912), p. 46.

24. R. E. Swartwout, *The Monastic Craftsman* (Cambridge, 1932), pp. 35–36.

25. *On Painting*, trans. John R. Spencer (New Haven, 1956), pp. 74–75.

26. *Ibid.*, p. 80.

27. Bernard S. Myers, *Modern Art in the Making* (New York, 1950), p. 367.

28. R. B. Blakeney, *Meister Eckhardt* (New York, 1957), p. 206.

The Smile of the Buddha

1. S. Radhakrishnan, *Indian Philosophy* (London, 1948), I, 341–475.

2. E. G. Thomas, *The Life of Buddha as Legend and History* (London, 1952), pp. 66–67.

3. *Ibid.*, p. 89.

4. S. Radhakrishnan and C. A. Moore, eds., *A Source Book in Indian Philosophy* (Princeton, 1957), pp. 292–325.

5. Sir John Marshall, *The Buddhist Art of Gandhara* (Cambridge, 1960), pp. 7–8.

6. P. T. Young, *Emotion in Man and Animal* (New York, 1950), pp. 180–82, 252.

7. R. L. Illingsworth, *The Normal Child* (Boston, 1957), p. 211.

8. E. Bergler, *Laughter and the Sense of Humor* (New York, 1956), p. 49.

9. R. Spitz and K. M. Wolf, "The Smiling Response," *Genetic Psychology Monographs*, No. 34 (1946), pp. 57–125.

10. Young, *op. cit.*, p. 25.

11. G. W. Allport, *Personality, a Psychological Interpretation* (New York, 1937), p. 484.

12. S. A. Kinnier Wilson, *Neurology*, 2nd ed. (London, 1954), pp. 941–67.

13. Thomas, *op. cit.*, Chap. VI, "Austerities and Enlightenments."

14. E. Rowland, Jr., *The Evolution of the Buddha Image* (New York, 1963).

15. G. M. A. Richter, *Archaic Greek Art* (New York, 1949), Figs. 20, 81, 207, 208.

16. G. M. A. Richter, *Kouroi* (New York, 1942), pp. 3–4.

17. M. Bieber, *The Sculpture of the Hellenistic Age* (New York, 1955).

18. J. Dowson, *A Classical Dictionary of Hindu Mythology and Religion* (London, 1879), p. 373.

19. Isa Upanishad, 1:2; Mundaka Upanishad, 3, 2:6; R. E. Hume, *The Thirteen Principal Upanishads* (Madras, 1949), p. 346.

20. *Ibid.*, Brihad-Aranyaka Upanishad, 1, 5:23; 2, 4:13; 4, 3:35.

21. *Ibid.*, pp. 344–45.

22. E. Benkard, *Das Ewige Antlitz* (Berlin, 1927), Plate 96.

23. The author would like to thank Doctors Emory Klein and Béla Marquit of New York for their kind assistance in the anatomical analysis of the smile.

24. There are exceptions, such as the smiling head from the Apsidial Temple in Sirkap, first century A.D., which has a smile (Marshall, *op. cit.*, Fig. 36). But it portrays neither the Buddha nor a Bodhisattva, as the hairdress and headgear, which are typical of the Parthian nobility, indicate. This smiling female head may be either of a wealthy aristocratic devotee of Buddhism or, more likely, of a patroness of the temple (Marshall, *op. cit.*, pp. 30–31). Contemporary heads of Bodhisattvas found on the same site do not smile and have, with one exception, the mustache and turban (Marshall, *op. cit.*, Figs. 37–39). Other free-standing Buddhas have mild expressions and hidden or implicit smiles (Marshall, *op. cit.*, Figs. 132–34). Since their *buccinators* are contracted and the eyes are half open, so as to convey the impression of squinting, some scholars have been led to read more into the expression than was actually intended. The *anguli oris* are not lifted up, and the *rima oris* is horizontal, if not curved down slightly. There are additional free-standing sculptures which may be said to be very grave, with wide-open eyes and depressed *anguli oris* (Marshall, *op. cit.*, Figs. 85, 86, 131).

25. Rowland, *op. cit.*, p. 12.

26. Marshall, *op. cit.*, Figs. 61, 63, 67.

27. Laws VII: 803c.

Allegories of the Gothic Cathedral

1. R. Krautheimer, "Introduction to an Iconography of Mediaeval Architecture," *Journal of the Warburg and Courtauld Institutes*, V (London, 1942); A. Grabar, *Martyrium* (Paris, 1943–1946); S. Guyer, *Grundlagen Mittelalterlicher Abendländischer Baukunst* (Zurich, 1950); H. Sedlmayr, *Die Entstehung der Kathedrale*. (Zurich, 1950); E. Panofsky, *Gothic Architecture and Scholasticism* (Latrobe, Pa., 1951); Otto Von Simson, *The Gothic Cathedral* (New York, 1956).

2. Lynn Thorndike, *A History of Magic and Experimental Science* (New York, 1958), II, 131; hereinafter cited as Thorndike II.

3. J. Kreuser, *Der Christliche Kirchenbau* (Regensburg, 1860), I, 731; cf. O. Von Simson, *op. cit.*, pp. 8–13.

NOTES

4. W. Andrae, *Das Gotteshaus* (Berlin, 1930); R. Patai, *Man and Temple* (London, 1947).

5. M. Eliade, *Patterns in Comparative Religion* (New York, 1958), pp. 367–85, 448.

6. W. Ganzenmüller, *Das Naturgefühl im Mittelalter* (Leipzig, 1914) is a prime source of poetic yet keen and scientific nature observations by medieval scholars, mystics, and travelers.

7. *Ibid.*

8. J. K. Wright, *The Geographical Lore of the Time of the Crusaders* (New York, 1925), pp. 218–19.

9. F. Gribble, *The Early Mountaineers* (London, 1899), pp. 14–17.

10. *Ibid.*, p. 45.

11. *Mediaeval Art* (New York, 1942), p. 16.

12. Thorndike II, 156.

13. Wright, *op. cit.*, pp. 323–24.

14. E. Panofsky, *Abbot Suger* (Princeton, 1948), p. 61; cf. R. E. Swartwout, *The Monastic Craftsman* (Cambridge, Eng., 1932), VIII-IX.

15. A. C. Crombie, *Augustine to Galileo* (Cambridge, Mass., 1953), pp. 91–92.

16. Panofsky, *op. cit.*, p. 63.

17. Crombie, *op. cit.*, p. 95.

18. Thorndike II, 424–25, 427.

19. Thorndike II, 566.

20. Thorndike II, 556.

21. Thorndike, II, 452, 468.

22. Thorndike II, 589–90.

23. *Studies in the History of Mediaeval Science* (Cambridge, Mass., 1924), p. 19.

24. Thorndike II, 565–66.

25. Thorndike II, 588.

26. Thorndike II, 832.

27. "Panegyric on the Building of Churches, Addressed to Pauline, Bishop of the Tyrians," *Ecc. Hist.* X, IV, 6–8.

28. John F. Fitchen, III, "A Comment on the Function of the Upper Flying Buttresses in French Gothic Architecture," *Gazette des Beaux-Arts*, Feb., 1955, 76.

29. *Ibid.*, pp. 69–90.

30. *Ibid.*, p. 82.

31. Francis Bond, *Gothic Architecture in England* (London, 1906), II, 372, 377.

32. Panofsky, *op. cit.*, p. 103.

33. "In some cases no doubt the grotesques may have been symbolical; the idea being that the Church overcomes and converts to good uses the most monstrous forms of evil." Bond, *op. cit.*, II, 399–400. L. B. Bridaham, following Emile Mâle, believes that religious and semireligious plays inspired many grotesque carvings. These include processions of monsters, as at the Fierté of Saint Romain, and similar processions with dragons at Rouen, Amiens, Noyon, Poitiers, Metz, and other places. *Gargoyle, Chimeras and the Grotesque in French Gothic Sculpture* (New York, 1930), pp. ix–xi.

34. Sedlmayr, *op. cit.*, p. 161.

35. *Butler's Lives of the Saints* (New York, 1956), I, 415–16.

36. Thorndike II, 466.

37. Thorndike II, 562.

38. Thorndike II, 657–58.

39. Thorndike II, 55.

40. G. J. Witkowski, *Les Licenses de l'Art Chrétien* (Paris, 1920); G. J. Witkowski, *L'Art Profane à l'Egise* (Paris, 1908); H. T. F. Rhodes, *The Satanic Mass* (London, 1954); C. G. Loomis, *White Magic* (Cambridge, 1948).

41. William Durandus, *The Symbolism of Churches and Church Ornaments* (London, 1906), pp. 17, 18.

42. K. J. Conant, in A. E. Bailey, ed., *The Arts and Religion* (New York, 1944), p. 75.

43. Krautheimer, *op. cit.*, p. 8.

44. *Loc. cit.*

45. Durandus, *op. cit.*, p. 20.

46. G. D'Alviella, *The Migration of Symbols* (Westminster, 1894), p. 150. For other cosmological interpretations and the origin of the rose window see W. Simpson, *The Buddhist Praying Wheel* (London, 1896); E. J. Beer, *Die Rose von Lausanne* (Berne, 1952); A. Rosenberg, *Die Christliche Bildmeditation* (München, 1955).

47. "On the Love of God," *Sermons on the Canticle of Canticles*, trans. T. L. Connolly (New York, 1937), pp. 156–57.

48. *Ibid.*, p. 193.

49. Paul Frankl, "The 'Crazy' Vaults of Lincoln Cathedral," *Art Bulletin*, XXXV, No. 2 (June, 1953), 102.

50. Nave and navel both relate to the Sanskrit *nabhila* as well as to the Greek *omphalos*—navel, center of the earth—which was marked at the temple of Apollo by a marble boss. Underneath the allegory of the church as a ship tossed by the sea, dear to patristic writers, hides another symbol, of the church as a male body in the sacred center. The connection between nave and navel, in other words, center of the earth as well as of the human body, is etymologically sound and more in agreement with St. John's vision. Cf. *The Oxford English Dictionary*, VII, p. 47.

51. Crombie, *op. cit.*, p. 210.

52. Thorndike II, 508.

53. Crombie, *op. cit.*, p. 198.

54. C. Singer, *A Short History of Anatomy* (New York, 1957), p. 68. This is a revised edition of Singer's *The Evolution of Anatomy* (1925).

55. Crombie, *op. cit.*, p. 149.

56. *Ibid.*, pp. 198, 206.

57. Singer, *op. cit.*, pp. 71–74.

58. *Ibid.*, pp. 74–78.

59. Yrjo Hirn, *The Sacred Shrine* (London, 1912), p. 450. The entire statement, however, reads as follows: "And let no one divert this [worship] to the Virgin Mary; Mary was the temple of God, not the God of the temple. And therefore He alone is to be worshipped who was working in His temple." "On the Holy Spirit," III, XI, *Nicene and Post Nicene Fathers, Second Series* (Grand Rapids, 1955), X, p. 146.

60. Hirn, *op. cit.*, p. 454.

61. *Ibid.*, pp. 456–57.

62. *The Library of Christian Classics* (Philadelphia, 1957), X, 202.

63. *The Library of Christian Classics*

NOTES

(Philadelphia, 1957), XIII, 123.

64. Panofsky, *op. cit.*, pp. 99, 103.

65. Durandus, *op. cit.*, pp. 12, 88.

66. J. Bute, *The Roman Breviary* (London, 1908), II, 633.

67. *Symbols of Christ* (New York, 1955), p. 72.

68. H. Jenner, *Christian Symbolism* (London, 1910), p. 39.

69. M. B. Freeman, "The Iconography of the Merode Altarpiece," *Metropolitan Museum of Art Bulletin*, December, 1957, pp. 133–34.

70. Hirn, *op. cit.*, p. 464.

71. *Ibid.*, pp. 331–49.

72. "In the fifteenth century people used to keep statuettes of the Virgin, of which the body opened and showed the Trinity within. The inventory of the treasure of the dukes of Burgundy makes mention of one made of gold inlaid with gems. Gerson saw one in the Carmelite monastery at Paris: he blames the brethren for it, not however, because such a coarse picture of the miracle shocked him as irreverent, but because of the heresy of representing the Trinity as the fruit of Mary." J. Huizinga, *The Waning of the Middle Ages* (London, 1952), p. 140.

73. E. Panofsky, *Early Netherlandish Painting* (Cambridge, 1953), II, Fig. 236.

74. *Ibid.*, I, p. 145.

75. *Ibid.*, II, p. 336.

76. *Mediaeval Church Vaulting* (Princeton, 1915), pp. 86–87.

77. H. Gray, *Anatomy of the Human Body*, 26th ed. (Philadelphia, 1956), pp. 451–52; Fig. 451, p. 462.

Symbol or Visual Presence?

1. *A Select Library of Nicene and Post-Nicene Fathers, of the Christian Church, Second Series* (Grand Rapids, 1956), XIV, 554.

2. Robert Goldwater and Marco Treves, *Artists on Art* (New York, 1947), p. 361.

3. *Images and Symbols* (New York, 1961), p. 172.

4. New York, 1963, p. 160.

5. *Ibid.*, p. 169.

6. "Exhortation to the Heathen," IV, *The Ante-Nicene Fathers* (Grand Rapids, 1951), II, 188.

7. Herbert Read and Edward Dahlberg, *Truth Is More Sacred* (London, 1961), p. 27.

8. Goldwater and Treves, *op. cit.*, p. 375.

The Symbolism of Nonobjective Art

1. "De Profundis," *The Works of Oscar Wilde*, ed. G. F. Maine (New York, 1954), p. 864.

2. *The Brotherhood of Religions* (Bombay, 1944), p. 27.

3. American edition, ed. Hilla Rebay (New York, 1946), pp. 26–27.

4. She was exposed by the London

Society of Psychical Research "as
one of the most accomplished, ingenious
and interesting impostors in history."
E. M. Butler, *The Myth of the Magus*
(Cambridge, Eng., 1948), p. 247; cf. G. M.
Williams, *Priestess of the Occult* (New
York, 1946).

5. Kandinsky, *op. cit.*, p. 17.

6. Michel Seuphor, *Piet Mondrian*
(New York, 1956), pp. 54–58.

7. Michel Seuphor, "Piet Mondrian:
1914–18," *Magazine of Art*, May, 1952, p.
223.

8. *Ibid.*, p. 217.

9. H. L. C. Jaffé, *De Stijl* (Amsterdam,
1956), pp. 220–22.

10. *Ibid.*, p. 224.

11. Seuphor, *Piet Mondrian*, p. 118.

12. R. E. Hume, *The Thirteen Principal
Upanishads* (Madras, 1949), p. 404.

13. F. Edgerton, *The Bhagavad Gita*
(Cambridge, 1944), p. 111.

14. Lama Anagarika Govinda,
Grundlagen Tibetischer Mystik (Zurich,
1956), p. 199.

15. A. K. Gordon, *The Iconography
of Tibetan Lamaism* (Tokyo, 1959),
p. 27, n.1.

16. *Ibid.*, pp. 89–90.

17. Seuphor, *Piet Mondrian*, p. 118.

18. *Ibid.*, p. 36.

19. Jaffé, *op. cit.*, p. 217.

20. *Die Gegenstandslose Welt*,
Bauhausbücher No. 11 (Munich, 1927),
pp. 74, 82.

21. "What Abstract Art Means to Me,"
Museum of Modern Art Bulletin,
Spring, 1951, pp. 12–13.

22. Paul Tillich, *Dynamics of Faith*
(New York, 1957), p. 41.

23. *The Oxford English Dictionary*
(Oxford, 1933), X, p. 362. It is highly
doubtful, however, whether there is an
occult relationship between the symbol
and that which is being symbolized.
Jung, Tillich, and Maritain defend this
theory, while Ogden, Whitehead, and
Langer oppose it.

24. *Philosophy in a New Key* (New
York, 1948), p. 77.

25. B. C. Heyl, *New Bearings in
Esthetics and Art Criticism* (New Haven,
1952), pp. 74–77.

26. *Tractatus Logico-Philosophicus*
(London, 1955), p. 27.

Symbolism and Allegory

1. *The Symbolism of Churches and
Church Ornaments* (London, 1906),
pp. 62–63.

2. Florence McCulloch, *Mediaeval
Latin and French Bestiaries* (Chapel Hill,
1960), pp. 146–47.

3. The most famous painting with an
ostrich egg suspended in a church is Piero
Della Francesca's altarpiece portraying
the kneeling Duke Frederigo da Monfeltro
(c. 1474), now in the Brera in Milan.
CF. Millard Meiss, "Ovum Strunthionis,"
in *Studies in Art and Literature for
Belle da Costa Greene*, ed. D. Miner
(Princeton, 1954), pp. 92–101.

NOTES

4. "The primary difference between symbolism and allegory is that the former sees 'sermons in stone'; the latter from phantom stones builds sermons." C. R. Post, *Mediaeval Spanish Allegory*, pp. 4–5, quoted in H. Flanders Dunbar, *Symbolism in Mediaeval Thought* (New York, 1961), p. 279, n.115a.

5. *The Didascalicon of Hugh of St. Victor*, trans. Jerome Taylor (New York, 1961), pp. 145–46.

6. Yrjo Hirn, *The Sacred Shrine* (London, 1912), pp. 441–49.

7. J. Jules Lutz and Paul Perdrizet, *Speculum Humanae Salvationis* (Mülhausen, 1907–09), I, 271.

8. *Ibid.*, p. 3, lines 67–70.

9. Jean Adhemar, *Influences Antiques dans l'Art du Moyen Age Français*, Studies of the Warburg Institute, VII (London, 1939); cf. Jean Seznec, *The Survival of the Pagan Gods* (New York, 1953).

10. H. Jenner, *Christian Symbolism* (London, 1910), p. 38.

11. Joseph Campbell, in his book *The Hero with a Thousand Faces* (New York, 1949), argues for universal types of myths, which, however, are not allegories in the strict sense in which the term is employed here, but mythological heroes and adventures interpreted from a Jungian point of view.

12. *Symbolism of the Cross* (London, 1958), p. 14, n.3.

13. *Nature and Grace in Art* (Chapel Hill, 1964), p. 26.

14. Rollo May, *Symbolism in Religion and Literature* (New York, 1961), p. 20.

15. *Dementia Praecox or the Group of Schizophreneas*, trans. J. Zinkin (New York, 1950), p. 438, n.78.

16. *Interpretation of Schizophrenia* (New York, 1955), pp. 291–92.

17. *Magic and Schizophrenia* (New York, 1955), p. 166.

18. Quentin Lauer, *Phenomenology* (New York, 1965), p. 74.

19. *Essay on Man* (New Haven, 1962), p. 25.

A Sixfold Schema of Symbolism

1. Max Schlesinger, *Geschichte des Symbols* (Berlin, 1912), pp. 14, 19–20.

2. *Ancient Art and Ritual* (Oxford, 1948), p. 227.

3. *Problems of Art* (New York, 1957), p. 25.

4. *Christian Mysticism* (London, 1948), p. 5.

5. *A Select Library of Nicene and Post-Nicene Fathers of the Christian Church, Second Series* (Grand Rapids, 1956), XIV, 401.

6. Edwyn Bevan, *Holy Images* (London, 1940), p. 99.

7. *A Guide to Sanchi* (Delhi, 1955), p. 43.

8. *See* "The Symbolism of Nonobjective Art," pp. 106–18 of this book.

9. W. Kandinsky, *On the Spiritual in Art*, ed. Hilla Rebay (New York, 1946);

NOTES

Michel Seuphor, *Piet Mondrian* (New York, 1956); H. L. C. Jaffé, *De Stijl* (Amsterdam, 1956).

10. R. E. Hume, *The Thirteen Principal Upanishads* (Madras, 1949), p. 439.

11. *Images and Symbols* (New York, 1961), pp. 62, 177.

12. G. E. Rolt, *Dionysius the Aeropagite* (London, 1940), p. 67.

13. *The Fathers of the Church* (New York, 1953), V, 252–53.

14. Rolt, *op. cit.*, p. 51.

15. *Ibid.*, p. 194.

16. Edwyn Bevan, *Symbolism and Belief* (London, 1938), p. 20.

17. Jack Finegan, *Light From the Ancient Past* (Princeton, 1947), p. 382.

18. *Ibid.*

19. *Jewish Symbols in the Greco-Roman Period* (New York, 1956), V, 3–4, 10.

20. Goodenough, *op. cit.*, IV, 38; V, 48–49.

21. The Temple of Solomon contained carvings of gourds, flowers, palm trees, two seraphim in the inner sanctuary, two bronze pillars with pomegranate and lily decorations, twelve oxen to support the molten sea, but no fish. Cf. I Kings 7ff.

22. Odell Shepard, *The Lore of the Unicorn* (New York, 1930), pp. 27–28.

23. *Ibid.*, p. 47.

24. *Ibid.*, pp. 49, 50–55.

25. *Ibid.*, p. 94.

The Eclipse of Symbolism

1. Alfred Lehmann, *Aberglaube und Zauberei* (Stuttgart, 1898); R. C. Thompson, *Semitic Magic* (London, 1908); W. J. Perry, *The Origin of Magic and Religion* (London, 1923).

2. *Magic, Science and Religion* (Boston, 1948), pp. 56–57.

3. *Magic and Schizophrenia* (New York, 1955), p. 11.

4. *Shamanism* (New York, 1964), p. xix. Cf. Mircea Eliade, *The Sacred and the Profane* (New York, 1959).

5. Richard Chase, *Quest for Myth* (Baton Rouge, 1949), p. 78.

6. "Exhortation to the Heathen," IV, *The Ante Nicene Fathers*, (Grand Rapids, 1951), II, 191.

7. *Ibid.*, p. 192.

8. C. K. Ogden, and I. A. Richards, *The Meaning of Meaning* (New York, 1952), p. 266.

9. "Exhortation to the Heathen," X, *The Ante Nicene Fathers*, II, 200.

10. George Boas, trans. (Indianapolis, 1953), pp. 8, 14.

11. H. Shapley and H. E. Howarth, *A Source Book in Astronomy* (New York, 1929), pp. 1–2.

12. E. Rosen, *Three Copernican Treatises* (New York, 1939), pp. 147–48.

Index

INDEX

INDEX

Ekkehard, 49
El Greco, 25
Eliade, Mircea, 102, 136, 151–52
Ensor, James, 51
Erigena, John Scotus, 136
Essenes, 47
Etruscan art, 56; sarcophagus from
   Caere, 62, 16
Eusebius, 76
Expressionism, 51, 113
Eyes, as symbols, in Iranian mythology,
   37–38; in Hindu and Buddhist philosophy,
   38, 45–46, 8; in Egyptian art, 39–41; in
   Greek mythology, 41–42; among the
   Mesopotamians, 43–44, 46; in Christian
   art, 47–48; in Byzantine-oriental art,
   47–48; in the Gothic period, 49; during
   the Renaissance, 49; in modern art, 49–51

F

Fertility goddesses, 38–39, 149
Fitchen, John F., III, 77
Flammarion, Nicholas, 107
Fox, George, 136
Francesca, Piero della, 25
Francis of Assisi, St., 90
Frankfort, Henry, 36
Frankl, Paul, 88
Frazer, Sir James, 39
Frederick II, 89

G

Galen, 89
Gandhara sculptures. *See* Buddhist art
Gaster, Theodore, 30
Georgio, Francesco di, 83
Gerald of Cremona, 89
Gilgamesh epic, 33, 34
Giorgione, 25
Goodenough, Erwin R., 141

Gothic cathedral, beginnings, 67–68; as a
   sacred city, 69–70; exteriors, 70, 75, 79–80;
   locations, 76–77; flying buttresses, 77–78;
   gargoyles and grotesques, 81; entrances
   and interiors, 83, 86–87; and the body of
   Christ, 84–86, 22(a); ribbed vaulting in,
   88, 93–95, 26; relationship to human
   anatomy, 88–89, 92–93; and Virgin
   Mary, 90–95, 23, 24, 25
Greek art, motifs of, 24–25; mythology in,
   34, 38–39; treatment of eyes, 41–42, 6;
   Archaic, 41–42, 56, 57, 58, 59, 13;
   Hellenistic, 41–42, 48, 58; stylistic
   traditions of, 47–48
Grosseteste, Robert, 74
Guénon, René, 126
Gupta style, in Buddhist art, 64, 65

H

Hali Abbas, 89
Hammurabi, Stele of, 23
Harrison, Jane, 130
Haskins, C. H., 75
Hebrews, and images, 23–24, 31–34, 153, 156
Hellenistic art. *See* Greek art
Hildegarde of Bingen, St., 68, 144
Hindu philosophy, and the eye, 38; and
   death, 59; and the smile, 64; influence
   on Theosophy, 107, 110
Hofmann, Hans, on the act of painting, 28
Hugh of Lucca, 89
Hugh of St. Victor, 68, 123

I

Ikhnaton, 40
Images, Egyptian, 21, 35–36; in Old
   Testament, 31–33; Sumerian, 33;
   Babylonian, 33; Greek, 34; in medieval
   art, 48–49; Buddhist, 52–60 *passim*; powers
   of, 103. *See also* Symbolism

INDEX

INDEX

in, 81–82; and light as symbol, 87; and the fish as symbol, 140–41

Nolde, Emil, 51

Nonobjective art, and the creative process, 28; and mysticism of, 111–14, 135–36; styles of, 113; contributions of, 116; critics of 118; imagery of, 134

O

Old Testament, 121; and creation, 30–31; prophecies, 70; Satan in, 81; Song of Solomon, 123; and the fish as symbol, 141–42

Osiris, 22, 131

Ovid, 35, 38

P

Painting, ancient, 22; communication of, 101–2; representational *vs.* nonobjective, 113, 114

Pala style, in Buddhist art, 65

Paleolithic period, symbols of, 19–20, 38, 149, 152; position of artist in, 29–30

Panofsky, Erwin, 93–94

Paul, apostle, 153

Peter III, King of Aragon, 71

Petit, Jean, 123

Photius, 144, 153

Picasso, Pablo, 51, 103

Plato, on Egyptian art, 18; on artists, 29, 36; quoted, 66; on painting, 101; world view of, 153–54, 155

Pliny, 72

Plotinus, 136, 138

Pollock, Jackson, 114, 116; "#5, 1950," 29

Pottery, in ancient art, 31, 36, 1

Prehistoric caves, French and Spanish, 17; symbols, 19–20

Primitive societies, art motifs of, 17–20

Ptolemy of Lucca, 74

R

Read, Sir Herbert, 36, 104

Redon, Odilon, 102

Rembrandt van Rijn, 135

Renaissance art, motifs of, 25

Rhazes, 89

Rheims, cathedral of, 77, 82, 21

Rheticus, George Joachim, 156

Ristolo d'Arezzo, 73

Roger of Salerno, 89

Róheim, Géza, 128; quoted, 151

Romanesque art, 48; cathedrals, 68, 83, 88

S

Sacred and the Profane, concept of, 151–52, 156

Schöner, John, 156

Science, advances of, 27; relationship to symbolism, 128, 154–55, 156

Scriabin, Alexander, 107

Sculpture, ancient, 22; Egyptian, 40; Greek, 41–42, 58; Hindu and Buddhist, 56–66 *passim*

Seurat, Georges, 105

Shoenmakers, M. H. J., 108

Smile, in Buddhist art, 52–66 *passim*; as universal symbol, 54; psychology of, 54–56; in Greek art, 56, 57–58; in Etruscan art, 62; morphology of, 62, 65

Socrates, 101, 153

Spitz, René, 54–56

Steiner, Rudolph, 107

Stephen of Antioch, 89

Styles, in art, Buddhist, 45–46; Byzantine-oriental, 48; Hellenistic, 48, 58–59; Gothic, 48, 67–68, 96; Romanesque, 48, 96; nonobjective, 111–13; historical, 134–35

Suger, Abbot, 68, 72, 73, 74, 80

Surrealism, 51, 113

INDEX

Suso, St., 49

Symbolism, and Paleolithic man, 19–20; of Egyptian art, 21–23; in nonobjective art, 27–28, 113–18, 135–36; and aesthetics, 101–3; and the cross, 105, 27; and metasymbolism, 116–18, 134, 135; classes of symbols, 120–21; and allegory, 121–25; and various cultures, 126–27; dangers of, 127–28; in schizophrenics, 128; etymology of "symbol," 129; interpretations, 130; transformations in, 131–33; and mystics, 136–38; the fish in, 139–42, *33*; the unicorn in, 142–47; hierarchy of, 147–48; belief in, 150–51; and medieval society, 154; and science, 154–56. *See also* Eyes, as symbols; Gothic cathedral; Smile, in Buddhist art

T

Thaddeus of Florence, 89

Theosophy, origins, 106–7; influence on modern art, 108, 110

Thomas à Kempis, 136

Tillich, Paul, on symbolism, 126–27

Tuotilo, 49

U

Unicorn myth, 145–47, *34, 35*

Upanishads, 110, 136; on death, 59–60

V

Van Der Leeuw, Gerardus, 103

Van Eyck, Jan, 93

Venus statuettes, 19–20, 38–39

Vesalius, 90

Vincent of Beauvais, 74, 82

Viollet-Le-Duc, Eugène, 68, 77

Virgin of Nôtre Dame, Paris, 124–26, *32*

Vishmakarman, 30

Vitruvius, 83–84

W

Wadia, Sophia, 107

Walpurga, St., 81

Ward, Clarence, 95

Wei sculptures, in Buddhist art, 64–65

Wilde, Oscar, 106

William of Saliceto, 89

Winzen, Damasus, 91

Wittgenstein, Ludwig, 118

Wolf, K. M., 54–56

Z

Zen Buddhism, 113